The Hand Me Down Cookbook is a selected variety of food with a special touch for everyday cooking. It includes many handed down recipes from grandmother and friends, and a selection of dishes you find in restaurants, but want to know how to make at home. Instructions are simple, easy to follow and complete. Approximately sixty on hand ingredients are all you need to use *The Hand Me Down Cookbook.* You won't need to run to the store for something you'll use just once.

Mostly though, it is designed for you to make your own.
Write in it.
Add your own handed down recipes to it.
The pages and white space have been put there especially for you.
Start your own collection in this book and make it your own hand me down cookbook.

Here's a sample of what you'll find among the 200 recipes:

Miscellaneous: curry powder, peach chutney, stuffed grape leaves, graham crackers, noodles, beef jerky, rum truffles
Soup: Greek lemon soup, cream of broccoli
Salad: Caesar salad, three bean salad
Entrees: crab quiche, fettucini
Meat: stuffed flank steak, orange pork roast
Chicken: Moroccan chicken, picnic chicken
Fish: sole Marguery, cioppino
Vegetables: tomatoes with shallots, potato pancakes
Breads: Pita bread, brown bread
Cakes and Cookies: ginger snaps, chocolate orange cake
Desserts: crepes Suzette, chocolate roll

The Hand Me Down Cookbook

collected by Eleanor Evans

Two Step Books   Berkeley   California

Library of Congress Cataloging in Publication Data

Evans, Eleanor, 1932-
    The Hand Me Down Cookbook
    includes index
    1. Cookery I. Title
Tx715.e8823   641.5   78.2935

ISBN 0-931018-00-5

Special thanks to Laura Ashley Inc. for supplying the
wallpaper from which the cover was designed.

Printed in the United States of America

Published by Two Step Books
2490 Channing Way #210, Berkeley, California

To my mother and the friends who gave me these recipes
and especially Liza who put it together.

For Stacey, Holly, Marcy, Lindsey, Mark and Sam.

Contents

miscellaneous

Artichoke Appetizer

2 jars marinated artichoke hearts (6 oz. each)
1 clove garlic, minced
1 small onion, finely chopped
4 eggs
¼ cup dry bread crumbs
¼ tsp. salt
⅛ tsp. oregano
⅛ pepper
½ lb. Cheddar cheese, shredded
2 tbsp. parsley

Drain 1 jar of artichokes and put marinade in a skillet. Drain the other jar and chop all artichokes. Set aside.

Sauté onion and garlic in marinade for 5 minutes. Beat eggs in a medium bowl, add crumbs and seasonings. Stir in cheese, parsley, artichokes and onions. Pour into greased 8″ by 8″ baking pan and bake at 325° for 30 minutes or until eggs are set. Cool in pan and cut into small squares.

Eggplant Appetizer

1 small eggplant
⅔ cup chopped onion
1 clove garlic, minced
4 mushrooms, halved and thinly sliced
¼ cup olive oil
2 to 3 tbsp. vegetable oil
4 tbsp. tomato paste
1 tbsp. lemon juice
1 tsp. salt
2 tbsp. red wine vinegar
1 tsp. brown sugar
2 tsp. capers (optional)
¼ cup water
8 to 10 sliced stuffed green olives

Chop eggplant into quarter inch cubes. Sauté garlic, onions and mushrooms in olive oil. Add eggplant and cook, stirring often, over low heat for 5 minutes. Add vegetable oil and continue to cook for 25 to 30 minutes more. Watch to make sure mixture does not stick or burn. Cook until eggplant is soft.

Combine all other ingredients (except olives) in a small bowl. Stir into eggplant mixture and cook 1 to 2 minutes. Remove from heat, add olives and chill. Serve with crackers.

Stuffed Grape Leaves
These can be served hot as an entree
or cold as an appetizer.

1 lb. lean ground meat (beef or lamb or half and half)
1 onion, finely chopped
½ cup uncooked rice
⅓ cup hulled, unroasted sunflower seeds or pine nuts
2 tbsp. dried dill
1 tbsp. lemon juice
2 tbsp. tomato paste
¾ cup water
¼ cup olive oil
1 jar grape leaves

Sauté onion in oil, add meat, cook until crumbly. Add rice, sunflower seeds, water, lemon juice and tomato paste. Simmer, stirring occasionally for 10 minutes or until water is gone. Cool.

Wash grape leaves in hot water and drain. Put 1 tbsp. of meat mixture on leaf, fold in edges like an envelope and roll up into finger shaped rolls.

Layer bottom of saucepan with imperfect leaves, pack stuffed grape leaves in layers. Add water to cover all but top layer. Place small plate on leaves upside down to prevent them from unrolling during cooking time. Bring to a boil, reduce heat and simmer for ½ hour or until water is gone.

Crab Mousse

Serve on crackers or thinly sliced
French bread as an appetizer.

12 oz. crab meat
1 cup celery, chopped fine
1 cup mayonnaise
⅓ cup finely chopped onion
1 8 oz. plus 1 3 oz. package cream cheese
1 can cream of mushroom soup*
1 envelope plain gelatin dissolved in ¼ cup hot water

Put cream cheese, soup and onion in large saucepan; heat stirring until cheese melts. Add gelatin and mix. Remove from heat. Add crab, celery, mayonnaise and blend. Chill 4 hours or more.

*Or your own.

Pate

Serve warm with French bread or Melba toast,
or press into mold lined with lightly greased
wax paper, chill and slice. This is a coarse pate.
If you prefer a smoother texture, it can be put in
the blender.

½ lb. chicken livers
4 to 5 mushrooms, finely chopped
2 to 3 green onions, finely chopped
   (including some green)
½ cup butter
4 tbsp. teriyaki sauce

Remove fat and tissues from livers. Coarsely chop. In
a heavy skillet sauté mushrooms and onions in half of
the butter. Push to one side and add the rest of the
butter. When butter foams, put in chicken livers and
cook stirring over low heat for 10 minutes, until done.
Stir livers, mushrooms and onions together, add
teriyaki sauce and stir cooking for 2 to 3 minutes
longer. Remove from heat and mash mixture with
wooden masher or fork.

Guacomole

2 ripe avocadoes
1 tbsp. lemon or lime juice
½ tsp. garlic salt
2 drops Tabasco sauce
1 small tomato, finely chopped

Peel and mash avocado. Add lemon juice, garlic salt, Tabasco and blend. Stir in tomato and chill. Leave the avocado seed in the guacomole to prevent it from turning dark. Use this as a dip, add it to tacos or top hamburgers with it.

Dip for Fresh Vegetables

1 cup sour cream
1 cup mayonnaise
1 tbsp. dried parsley
1 tbsp. dried chives
1 tsp. dried dill
1 tsp. Beau Monde seasoning

Mix all ingredients and chill. Serve with mushrooms, cauliflower, cherry tomatoes, carrots, green onions or other raw vegetables.

Chili con Queso
Serve this hot in a chafing dish with corn chips.

½ cup finely chopped onion
1 tsp. oil
2 green chilies, finely chopped
1 large ripe tomato, peeled and finely chopped
½ tsp. salt
3 tbsp. dry white wine
¾ lb. Cheddar cheese, grated

Sauté onions in oil. Add chilies, tomatoes, salt and white wine. Cook over low heat for 5 to 10 minutes. Add cheese and stir until melted.

Toasted Sunflower Seeds
Sunflower seeds are good sprinkled on salads, as a condiment with curry or for snacks.

2 cups hulled, unroasted sunflower seeds
3 tbsp. Kikkoman soy sauce

Heat a heavy skillet, put in sunflower seeds and stir constantly over medium heat until seeds are golden brown; 5 to 10 minutes. Turn heat off and sprinkle with soy sauce, stirring until seeds are coated and mixture is dry. Remove to plate to cool, store in covered jar.

Snacks

2 cups pretzels
2 cups rice chex
2 cups wheat chex
2 cups corn chex
1 to 1½ cups cashews
1 cup butter
¾ cup bacon grease
2 tsp. garlic salt
2 tsp. savory salt
2 tsp. celery salt
12 tsp. Worcestershire sauce
2 tsp. Tabasco sauce

Mix pretzels, cereal and nuts together in a large roaster. Melt butter, bacon grease and seasonings together in a saucepan. Pour over mixture in roaster and stir well. Heat one hour in a 200° oven, stirring often.

Beef Jerky

1½ lbs. flank steak
½ cup soy sauce
lemon pepper and garlic salt to taste

Cut off any excess fat. Cut flank steak across the grain into thin strips: 3 to 4 inches long. Strips should be about ¼ inch thick and ¾ inch wide. Put meat into a bowl with soy sauce and stir with a fork until sauce is absorbed.

Place a rack onto a cookie sheet or pan. (You can use a cake cooling or refrigerator rack.) Put meat strips onto rack in rows. Sprinkle both sides with lemon pepper and garlic salt. Use less if you like a mild jerky and more if you like it spicier. Place meat in a low oven (150° or less) for eight to ten hours or until jerky is dry but not brittle. Store in a covered container in the refrigerator.

Graham Crackers

2 cups whole wheat or graham flour
¾ cup white flour
1 tsp. baking powder
½ tsp. baking soda
¼ cup butter
¼ cup shortening
1 cup packed brown sugar
½ tsp. salt
½ cup milk (or buttermilk)
1 tsp. vanilla

Mix flours, baking powder and baking soda together and set aside. Cream butter, shortening, sugar and salt until fluffy. Alternately add flour mixture and milk to butter/sugar mixture. (You may decide it's easier to use your hands when the dough becomes stiff.)

Divide dough into quarters or workable sizes. On floured board, roll each quarter to 1/8 inch thick. Cut into desired shapes. You can make the crackers square, rectangular, or circular. If you want circles, use a cookie cutter or tin can to cut dough. Otherwise you can use a sharp knife. Put crackers on a greased cookie sheet and bake in a preheated 350° oven for 10 to 12 minutes.

French Toast

6 slices stale sourdough French bread
3 eggs
2 tsp. warm water
¼ tsp. vanilla

Put water in eggs, whip with wire whisk until thick but not foamy. Add vanilla. Soak bread in eggs on both sides. Fry in butter with a few drops of oil to prevent burning, in skillet, until brown on both sides. Sprinkle with powdered sugar when serving.

Chicken Salad for Sandwiches
Avocado slices are excellent in this sandwich.

2 cups chicken breasts, cooked and chopped
¾ cup celery, finely chopped
3 tbsp. lemon juice
1 tsp. coarsely ground black pepper
¼ tsp. salt
mayonnaise

Mix chicken and celery, sprinkle lemon juice, salt and pepper over chicken, mix well. Stir in enough mayonnaise to hold filling together. You can substitute 2 tsp. lemon pepper for the lemon juice and pepper (leave out the salt).

Baked Beans

Here is a way to make canned beans taste like the old fashioned slow cooked ones, if you don't have the inclination to make them from scratch.

1 large can B and M baked beans (1 lb. 12 oz.)
5 tbsp. catsup
⅔ to ¾ cup firmly packed brown sugar
5 to 6 slices onion, sliced very thin
2 to 3 slices bacon, raw

Put beans in a buttered casserole, discard pork fat. Stir in catsup and brown sugar. Place a layer of onion on top, top with bacon. (Cut pieces in half to make them fit.) Bake for 30 minutes at 425°, turn oven down to 350° and bake for 1 to 1½ hours until the sauce is thick. Serves four to six.

Noodles
Fresh noodles are easy and delicious.

2 cups flour
2 eggs
¼ tsp. salt
2 tbsp. olive oil

Sift flour into bowl, make a well in the center and break in eggs. Stir quickly with a fork. Add salt and oil and work flour in with your hands. If dough is too stiff, add to 2 tsp. warm water. Knead dough until smooth and elastic; about 15 minutes. Shape into a rectangle and roll very thin on a lightly floured board. (This is good for your stomach muscles.) Lightly dust with flour and roll up like a jelly roll. Cut very thin slices for fettucine and wide slices for regular noodles. Shake out noodles to unroll, put on plate and cover with a tea towel for an hour or until ready to use. Cook in boiling salted water until just tender.

Plain Dumplings
These can be put in stews, or stewed chicken.

1½ cups flour
1 tsp. salt
1½ tsp. baking powder
1 tbsp. butter
1 egg
1 cup milk

Sift flour, salt and baking powder together in a bowl. Blend in butter with a fork, or pastry blender; add milk and egg and stir well. Drop into pot from a tablespoon, but first remove pot from heat. Never put dumplings in boiling liquid and do not let them settle into the liquid. Cover and put back on heat and simmer for 20 minutes. Do not lift the lid.

Chili Sauce

12 large, very ripe tomatoes
4 green peppers
4 large onions
2 tbsp. salt
1 cup sugar
3 cups apple cider vinegar

Pour boiling water over tomatoes to make them easy to peel; peel and cut into quarters. Put them in a large heavy pot, mash with a potato masher.

Seed green peppers and put them through a food grinder. Peel onions and put through a food grinder. Add peppers, onions, salt, sugar and vinegar to tomatoes, stir well. Bring to a boil, turn heat down and simmer until thick and well cooked; 2 to 3 hours. Stir occasionally. Sauce should be reduced by one half.

Sterilize jars in boiling water for 10 minutes, fill hot jars with hot chili sauce and seal with melted parrafin or self sealing lids. Makes 2½ to 3 quarts.

Use with meat loaf, cold meats or as a topping for hamburgers. A few tablespoons mixed with mayonnaise, a chopped, boiled egg and a little lemon juice makes a good Thousand Island dressing.

Chinese Plum Sauce

1 cup plums
1 cup apricots (if apricots are not in season,
you can use half canned and half dried)
1 cup sugar
½ cup apple cider vinegar
½ cup applesauce
2 tsp. diced ginger root (or candied ginger)

Pit and peel fruit. Chop.

Mix all ingredients together in a large kettle, bring to a boil. Turn heat down and simmer for one hour or until mixture is thick. Pour into hot sterilized jars while mixture is warm. Store one month in cool dark place.

Spiced Peaches

8 lbs. peaches
1 pint apple cider vinegar
4 lbs. sugar
3 to 4 sticks cinnamon
whole cloves

Pour boiling water over peaches to make them easy to peel; peel. If they are large, cut them in half, small ones can go into the jars whole. Stick 2 or 3 cloves in each peach.

Mix sugar and vinegar in a large kettle, bring to a boil, put peaches in and cook gently until peaches are tender; 5 to 10 minutes. Remove peaches to platter to cool. Put peaches in sterilized jars, pour cold syrup over them and let sit for 24 hours so that syrup thickens. Seal with parrafin or self sealing lids.

Peach Chutney

An outstanding chutney; use it with curry dishes, cold meats or as an accompaniment to cheese souffle, crab quiche or roast pork.

5 lbs. yellow peaches
2 lbs. brown sugar
juice of 1 lemon
½ tsp. salt
1 large onion, chopped
1 clove garlic, minced
½ cup preserved, crystallized ginger, finely chopped
2 mild green chili peppers, chopped
2 cups seedless raisins (half golden)
1 tsp. cinnamon
1 whole lemon peel and pulp, finely chopped
1¼ cups apple cider vinegar

Pour boiling water over peaches to make them easy to peel; peel and chop. Put in large kettle, mix in brown sugar and juice of 1 lemon. Bring to boil, cook for 15 minutes, stirring often.

Add remaining ingredients, mix well. Bring to a boil, turn heat down and simmer, stirring often until thick; 45 to 50 minutes. Put hot chutney into hot sterilized jars and seal with paraffin, or self sealing lids.

Never Fail Fudge

3 packages semisweet chocolate chips (6 oz. each)
1 can sweetened condensed milk
pinch of salt
1 ½ tsp. vanilla
½ cup chopped walnuts (optional)

Melt chocolate over very low heat. Stir once or twice. Remove from heat, add sweetened condensed milk, salt, vanilla and nuts. Stir only until smooth. Spread mixture evenly on buttered plate and chill until firm; about 2 hours. Cut into pieces and store covered.

Rum Truffles

1 6 oz. package semisweet chocolate chips
6 squares unsweetened baking chocolate
⅔ cup sweetened condensed milk
1 tbsp. rum

Melt chocolate in double boiler over hot water. Remove from heat and add sweetened condensed milk and rum. Stir until thickened. Cool and roll into balls. Roll balls into cocoa, chocolate decorettes, or finely crushed nuts.

Caramels

1 cup butter
1 lb. brown sugar
pinch of salt
1 cup light corn syrup
14 oz. sweetened condensed milk
1 tsp. vanilla

Melt butter over medium heat, add sugar and salt and mix well. Add milk and corn syrup, bring to a boil, stirring constantly. Turn heat down to medium and cook stirring constantly until candy thermometer reads 245°. Remove from heat and stir in vanilla. Pour into buttered 9 inch square pan, cool. Refrigerate until firm. Warm to room temperature before cutting.

Creamy Mints

3 oz. cream cheese, softened
2 cups powdered sugar, unsifted
2 to 3 drops peppermint flavoring

Soften and whip cream cheese with a wooden spoon. Blend in peppermint flavoring. Sift powdered sugar into cream cheese working it until it is well blended, kneading it with your hands. Press into small mint molds (which can be purchased at a kitchen store), or roll into small balls and press down with a fork. Roll lightly in granulated sugar.

Coffee Liqueur

3 cups sugar
4 cups water
2 oz. powdered instant coffee
1 vanilla bean
1 fifth inexpensive vodka

Mix sugar and water in a saucepan, bring to a boil. Boil 5 minutes. Remove from heat and stir in coffee. Cool. Put vodka and vanilla bean sliced lengthwise and cut into shorter pieces into the cooled syrup. Pour into sterilized half gallon bottle and let sit for 30 days. Upend the bottle occasionally. Strain into sterilized bottles and can or cork.

Irish Coffee

1 to 1½ tsp. sugar
¾ cup hot coffee
1 jigger Irish whiskey
stiffly whipped cream

Put sugar and whiskey in large cup or glass coffee cup, fill with hot coffee, stir to dissolve sugar. Put 1 to 2 tbsp. whipped cream on top, being careful to float the cream so it doesn't mix in. Serves one.

Gin Fizz

Fizzes are good to have with Eggs Benedict. They use up the extra egg whites.

2 tbsp. sugar
2 tbsp. lemon juice
⅓ cup heavy cream
2 jiggers gin
2 egg whites
¼ to ½ cup sparkling soda water
2 to 3 ice cubes

Put ice cubes in the blender to crush. Add sugar, lemon juice, cream, gin and egg whites. Blend at high speed until creamy and frothy. Add soda water, gently stir, and pour into glasses. Serves two.

Sangria

1 fifth red wine (Burgundy)
2 tbsp. brandy
juice of 2 oranges
juice of 1 lemon
½ cup sugar
8 oz. soda water

Put wine, brandy, sugar, orange and lemon juices in a large pitcher, stir well. Pour in the soda water and stir again. Serve over lots of ice.

Curry Powder

This is a mild sweet curry powder. For a hotter curry add ground chili peppers (not powder). Most curry powders start with coriander, turmeric, and cumin. (Some have fenugreek, also.) Cinnamon, cardamon, ginger, mace, paprika, mustard seed, fennel, allspice, cloves and nutmeg can be added. When using a pre-made curry powder, any of these spices may be added to make it sweeter: ginger, cinnamon, cardamon or a pinch of cloves. Experiment with different blends. The curry powder must be fried in butter to bring the flavor out; it cannot be put in after the liquids have been added. You can use either onions or tomatoes for the base.

3 tsp. coriander
2 tsp. turmeric
1½ tsp. ginger
1 tsp. cumin
1 tsp. cinnamon
½ tsp. mace
½ tsp. cardamon
½ tsp. allspice
¼ tsp. cloves

Mix all the spices together in a bowl. Let mixture sit for an hour or more so that the flavors blend. Store in a covered jar. Makes about 2 oz.

Vanilla

The quality of vanilla makes a big difference. To make a full flavored vanilla, put a vanilla bean sliced lengthwise into ½ pint rum or bourbon. It will turn into vanilla extract in 1 to 2 months. (Don't worry, it will not taste of rum or bourbon.) This is a strong vanilla: use less of it to taste.

To preserve fresh ginger root: scrub well, place in a small jar and cover with dry sherry. It will keep in the refrigerator without spoiling and can be used a little at a time.

Carbon knives keep a sharp edge longer than stainless steel ones, but will discolor unless wiped after each use. To remove stains, rub powdered cleanser on the blade with a cork.

Iron pans or steel omelet or crepe pans are wonderful to cook with, but need seasoning and care. Dry them on medium heat after each use, then lightly oil. If food sticks to pan, heat it, sprinkle with salt, and rub out with a paper towel. Discard the salt and lightly oil. This method will make other kinds of pans stick proof.

Two Modeling Doughs

One of these is baked, the other left to dry out. Christmas tree ornaments, etc. can be made with either. It is nice to have on hand for children to play with. Both will keep in the refrigerator in a plastic bag. If used this way, you can add one or two drops of oil of cloves or wintergreen as a preservative. (Available at a druggist.) Keep them out of reach though; they are highly toxic if drunk.

Dough One

1 cup flour
½ cup salt
½ cup water

Mix flour and salt in a bowl, gradually add water until dough is of the right consistency. Mix well and knead for 10 minutes. Bake at 325° for 30 minutes per ¼ inch of thickness. Let cool thoroughly before painting.

Dough Two

1 cup baking soda
½ cup cornstarch
½ cup plus 2 tbsp. cold water

Mix soda, cornstarch and cold water in a sauce pan. Boil 1 minute until it is the consistency of mashed potatoes. Turn out on waxed paper and knead for a few minutes. Shape and let dry for 24 to 48 hours before painting.

MISCELLANEOUS

MISCELLANEOUS

MISCELLANEOUS

MISCELLANEOUS

MISCELLANEOUS

MISCELLANEOUS

MISCELLANEOUS

soup

Greek Lemon Soup

4 cups chicken broth
2 tsp. butter
2 tbsp. uncooked rice
½ tsp. powdered chicken stock
¼ tsp. parsley
2 yolks or whole eggs
3 tbsp. lemon juice

In a saucepan, simmer covered chicken broth, butter, uncooked rice, chicken stock and parsley for 20 minutes.

Beat eggs in a small bowl until light. Add lemon juice and blend thoroughly.

When ready to serve, take one cup of soup and whip it into lemon juice and eggs. Pour this mixture into the remainder of the soup. Do not heat again. If the soup curdles, beat it with a wire whisk. Serves four.

French Onion Soup

4 medium sized onions, thinly sliced
4 tbsp. butter
4 cups beef stock
⅓ cup dry red wine
salt and pepper to taste
slices of French bread, toasted and quartered
grated Swiss cheese

In a large kettle melt butter, add onions and simmer for one hour, stirring frequently. Do not allow onions to brown.

Add beef stock and wine. Bring to a boil. Pour in individual bowls, topping each with one fourth slice of toast. Top each with 2 to 3 tbsp. grated cheese and place under broiler or in 400° oven until golden brown; about 3 minutes. Serve at once. Serves four.

Gazpacho

1 large cucumber, peeled and chopped
1 medium green pepper, seeded and chopped
4 medium tomatoes, quartered
3 green onions, chopped (white part only)
2 cloves garlic
3 small slices stale French bread (optional)
3 tsp. salt
6 tbsp. vinegar
3 tbsp. olive oil
1 cup water
2 cups tomato juice

Garnish

1 medium cucumber, peeled and chopped fine
1 medium green pepper, seeded and chopped fine
2 medium tomatoes, chopped fine
croutons (optional)

Place one half of everything except tomato juice and garnish in a blender. Blend well. Pour into a large bowl and repeat with remaining half. Mix thoroughly and chill well.

When ready to serve, stir in cold tomato juice. Top each bowl with garnish. Makes eight to nine cups.

Cream of Broccoli Soup

2 tbsp. butter
1 tbsp. onion, minced
1 tbsp. flour
2 cups chicken broth
1½ cups chopped broccoli
1 cup milk
¼ cup cream
salt and pepper to taste

Melt butter in a saucepan, add onion and cook until limp. Stir in flour. Set aside.

Cook broccoli in chicken stock until done. Strain stock into pan with butter/flour mixture. Bring to a boil, stirring with a wire whisk. Cook over medium heat for 5 minutes. Add milk and simmer, stirring for 5 to 10 minutes more.

Put half of the broccoli and soup in the blender and blend until well pureed. Pour into another pan and repeat with the second half. Blend together and heat. Just before serving, stir in the cream. Heat but do not boil. Serves two to four.

Potato and Leek Soup

2 leeks (½ lb.)
¼ cup onion, chopped
2 tbsp. butter
1 large potato (½ lb.)
2 cups chicken broth
¼ tsp. salt
1 cup milk
½ cup cream

Wash the leeks thoroughly. Cut off the dark green bottom, leaving some of the light green. Slice thinly. Heat butter in large saucepan or kettle. Sauté onions and leeks until limp: about 5 minutes.

Peel potatoes and cut into small cubes. Add chicken stock and salt to leeks in the saucepan, bring to a boil. Add potatoes. Turn heat down and simmer until potatoes are soft: 20 to 25 minutes.

Put half of the soup mixture in the blender and blend until well pureed. Repeat with the second half. Heat milk in a small saucepan. Pour it into the potato mixture, whipping with a wire whisk. Heat well, add cream, whipping again. Do not boil. Top each with chopped chives. Serves two to four. This may also be served very cold.

Oyster Stew

1 pint oysters
6 tbsp. butter
¼ tsp. salt
½ tsp. Worcestershire sauce
3 cups milk
1 cup cream
1 tbsp. butter
paprika

Heat oysters in their liquid. Add butter, salt and Worcestershire sauce, and heat until edges of oysters curl. (At this point the oysters can be cut into smaller pieces if desired.) Heat milk in another saucepan just until boiling. The edges will begin to bubble. Do not boil. Pour milk into oyster mixture. Add cream and heat. Do not boil. Serve in bowls, with a little butter on top and a light sprinkling of paprika. Serves two to four.

Oyster Soup

1½ stalks celery, finely chopped
½ medium onion, finely chopped
4 tbsp. butter
1 tsp. parsley
1 pint oysters, chopped (save liquid)
1 can consommé
1 cup water
sherry (optional)

Sauté celery and onions in butter until clear. Add chopped oysters and liquid, and cook until oysters are done; 5 minutes. Add consommé, water and parsley and simmer for 5 to 10 minutes. A teaspoon of sherry can be added to each bowl. Serves four.

Crab Soup

These ingredients may seem unappealing, but combine to make a very good soup.

2⅔ cups cream of tomato soup*
2⅔ cups split pea soup (without ham)**
1 to 2 tsp. sweet basil
⅓ to ½ lb. crab meat
sherry (optional)

Heat the soups together with basil. Do not boil. Add crab and heat for a few minutes longer. Put into soup dishes, add 1 tsp. sherry to each bowl. Serves four to six.

*Or 1 can tomato soup plus 1 can milk.
**Or 1 can split pea soup plus 1 can water.

Split Pea Soup with Ham

1 ham bone or ham hock
10 cups water
2 whole celery stalks
8 peppercorns
1 onion, finely chopped
2 cups quick cooking split peas

Put ham bone and cold water in a large kettle. (The cold water is what draws the flavor out.) Bring to a boil and skim. Add celery and peppercorns, simmer until meat is tender. Strain and remove meat from bone. Add meat, onions and peas to stock, bring to a boil and simmer covered for 1 hour and 15 minutes. Uncover and simmer for 20 minutes more. Slightly mash the peas. Serves eight.

Pistou

A hearty French soup; it is lighter and prettier than minestrone.

4 large carrots, diced
2 medium potatoes, diced
2 leeks, thinly sliced
4 tsp. salt
$\frac{1}{8}$ tsp. pepper
10 cups water
$\frac{1}{2}$ lb. fresh green beans, cut into 1 inch pieces
1 cup very thin spaghetti, broken into 3 inch lengths
$\frac{1}{2}$ cup soft bread crumbs
1 can red kidney beans (16 oz.)
$\frac{1}{2}$ cup olive oil or vegetable oil
$\frac{1}{4}$ cup fresh basil leaves, finely chopped or
    or 4$\frac{1}{2}$ tsp. dried crumbled basil*
$\frac{1}{4}$ cup tomato puree
3 cloves garlic, crushed
$\frac{1}{4}$ cup Parmesan cheese

Combine carrots, potatoes, leeks, salt and pepper and water in large kettle. Bring to a boil, cover and simmer one hour stirring occasionally.

Add green beans, spaghetti and bread crumbs, stir until crumbs blend in. Cover and simmer 15 minutes. Add kidney beans and simmer for 10 minutes more.

Just before serving, combine fresh basil, tomato puree and garlic in a soup tureen. Add cheese and oil, a few drops at a time, stirring until well combined. Add one cup of the hot soup, stirring well. Slowly add the rest. Serves six to eight.

*If using dried basil, crumble it into the oil and let sit for 15 minutes.

SOUP

salad

Spinach Salad

1 large bunch spinach
2 tomatoes, cut into wedges
2 hard boiled eggs, halved and sliced
2 fresh mushrooms, thinly sliced
5 slices bacon
4 green onions, chopped
3 tsp. sugar
⅓ cup tarragon wine vinegar

Wash spinach well, put in refrigerator to crisp.

Fry bacon slowly until well done. Drain on paper towel. Mix sugar and wine vinegar into bacon grease, heat until bubbly. Put in green onions and cook for 1 minute. Add tomatoes and mushrooms to spinach and pour on dressing. Add salt and pepper to taste and toss. Crumble bacon and sprinkle over salad. Add eggs and toss again.

This dressing can be used for German potato salad.

Caesar Salad
The tossing is the key to this salad.

1 head Romaine lettuce
1 cup plain croutons*
1 clove garlic
3 tbsp. olive oil
4 drops Worcestershire sauce
juice of ½ lemon
4 tbsp. olive oil
freshly ground black pepper
2 tbsp. grated Parmesan cheese
1 egg, coddled**

Wash and dry lettuce, crisp in refrigerator.

Put oil in skillet. Press garlic through garlic press into oil; heat to just warm. Add croutons and toss for 1 minute. Remove and set aside.

Rub a cut clove of garlic on inside of salad bowl. Break lettuce into bowl. Pour 2 tbsp. oil on lettuce and toss. Add pepper, 2 tbsp. oil and toss again. Mix Worcestershire sauce into lemon juice, pour on lettuce, break in egg and toss. Sprinkle cheese on salad and toss. Sprinkle on croutons and toss twice more.

*Croutons: cut French bread into small cubes, spread on greased cookie sheet, bake until crisp in 325° oven.

**To coddle egg: boil for not more than one minute. Remove from water.

Greek Salad

1 head Romaine lettuce
4 oz. Feta cheese
½ pint Greek black olives
2 tomatoes, cut into wedges
¼ cup sweet red onion rings
⅔ cup olive oil
⅓ cup red wine vinegar
¼ tsp. salt
½ to 1 tsp. dried oregano

Wash and dry lettuce; tear into small pieces and put in refrigerator to crisp.

Put oil, vinegar, salt and spices in a jar and shake well. Just before serving, crumble cheese over lettuce, add tomatoes and slices of onion. Pour on enough dressing to coat the leaves. Toss. Add olives and toss again.

Tabbouli Salad

Usually served with Romaine lettuce leaves; this is also good as an appetizer, or can be put in Pita bread with thin slices of roast beef.

1 cup cracked wheat bulgur
2 cups boiling water
2 tomatoes, finely diced
4 to 5 green onions, finely chopped
¾ to 1 cup fresh parsley, finely chopped
½ cup cucumber, finely chopped (optional)
2 cloves garlic, finely chopped
½ cup olive oil
½ cup lemon juice
2 tsp. salt

Place bulgur in bowl. Pour boiling water over it and let sit for 1 hour. Drain well, using fine strainer. Add tomatoes, green onions, parsley and cucumber. Mix oil, lemon juice, garlic and salt together and pour over bulgur. Stir well. Chill for at least two hours.

Three Bean Salad

1 can red kidney beans (27 oz.)
1 can garbanzo beans (15 oz.)
1 can cut green beans (16 oz.)
marinade
⅔ cup sugar
½ cup vegetable oil
½ cup red wine vinegar
1 clove garlic, finely minced
1 tsp. salt
½ cup onion, chopped

Combine marinade in a large bowl. Drain beans and put into marinade. Stir well. Refrigerate for at least 5 hours, stirring occasionally. Canned artichokes may be added.

Winter Salad

3 red apples
½ cup celery, chopped
½ cup grapes
¼ cup walnuts, coarsely chopped
mayonnaise

Core, do not peel apples. Cut into coarse sized pieces. Cut grapes in half and remove seeds. Mix apples, celery, and grapes together with enough mayonnaise to lightly coat. Add walnuts and serve on a lettuce leaf. Serves four.

Sweet Salad Dressing
Good with butter lettuce and avocado slices.

1 cup salad oil
⅓ cup apple cider vinegar
½ cup sugar
1 tbsp. dry mustard
1 tsp. salt
1 to 2 tsp. celery seed
3 tbsp. grated onion

Place all ingredients in blender; blend well. Make this a day ahead so the flavors will blend together.

Sherry Salad Dressing

1 quart mayonnaise
½ cup hot water
4 oz. blue cheese
¾ cup dry sherry
¼ clove garlic, minced

Place all ingredients in blender and blend until creamy.

Feta Salad Dressing

2 cups crumbled Feta cheese
2 cups mayonnaise
½ cup red wine vinegar
2 tbsp. olive oil
1 tsp. oregano
1 tbsp. Worcestershire sauce
2 cloves garlic, minced

Place all ingredients in a blender and blend until creamy. This dressing is good with any tossed green salad.

SALAD

SALAD

SALAD

Omelets

The trick to good omelets is to start cooking the eggs at a high heat. This will make them puff up. Then turn the heat down. Eggs are so easily cooked that their own heat will complete the cooking.

Farmers Omelet

2 eggs
1 tsp. warm water
¼ cup diced, cooked potato
1 green onion, chopped
2 to 3 slices bacon

Cook bacon, remove and drain on paper towel. Cook potatoes in bacon grease until golden brown. Add onion and quickly sauté. Set aside.

Whip eggs and water until well blended, not frothy. Heat the omelet pan, add a few drops of oil and 1 to 2 tsp. butter. When hot, pour in eggs, turning pan to coat the bottom. With a spatula pull egg from the edges toward the middle, turning the pan so the un-cooked egg goes to the side. Return to lower heat. Add bacon, potatoes, and onions to center of omelet and continue cooking until omelet is done. (A cover at this point will help them set.) Slide omelet onto plate and fold. Serves one.

Other omelet fillings

2 eggs
1 tsp. warm water
½ tsp. chopped chives, put into beaten eggs
2 tbsp. chopped onion
3 mushrooms, sliced
1 tbsp. butter
2 tbsp. chopped fresh tomato
2 tbsp. grated Swiss cheese

Sauté onions and mushrooms in butter, place on omelet, top with tomatoes and cheese, cover pan and cook until cheese has melted.

Leftover ratatouille or Chinese food make unusual omelet fillings.

Huevos Rancheros

4 to 6 eggs
4 to 6 tortillas
oil for frying tortillas
1 small onion, finely chopped
1 clove garlic, minced
2 tbsp. bacon grease or vegetable oil
1 can mild green chili peppers, seeded
    and chopped (4 oz.)
1 can tomatoes, chopped (save liquid) (1 lb.)
½ cup grated Cheddar cheese

Fry tortillas in hot oil on both sides until crisp and brown. Drain on paper towel.

Sauté onions and garlic in bacon grease. Stir in tomatoes (and liquid) and green chilies. Simmer for 10 to 15 minutes, stirring often. Poach eggs in the sauce, sprinkle with grated cheese, cover until cheese is melted. Serve on tortillas.

If you prefer a hotter sauce, add 1 tsp. chili powder with tomatoes.

Eggs Benedict

3 English muffins, split in half
6 slices of ham
6 poached eggs (Eggs can be poached and
   slipped into cold water immediately and
   reheated in hot water when ready to use.)
Hollandaise Sauce

Butter muffins and put under broiler until golden brown. Quickly fry ham and place on top of toasted muffins. Top each with a poached egg and Hollandaise sauce. Makes six.

Blender Hollandaise Sauce

3 egg yolks
2 to 3 tbsp. lemon juice
dash of salt
½ cup butter

Place egg yolks, salt and lemon juice in blender and blend for 1 minute. Melt butter in a small saucepan on low heat until bubbly. Slowly pour hot butter into egg yolks in blender, blend at high speed until sauce is thick. (This takes about 1 minute.) Serve immediately.

Two Yolk Hollandaise Sauce

Use this when making four servings instead of six.

2 egg yolks
¼ tsp. warm water
⅓ cup butter (5½ tbsp.)
1 tbsp. lemon juice

In a small deep bowl (not metal) whip egg yolks and water with a wire whisk until thick and lemon colored. This takes 2 to 3 minutes. In a small saucepan (not aluminum) heat butter and lemon juice on low heat until butter has melted and is bubbly. Slowly pour heated butter in a thin stream into egg yolks, whipping with whisk constantly. Whip until thickened; 2 to 4 minutes. Serve immediately. Makes ¾ cup.

Eggs Florentine

Top toasted English muffins with creamed spinach (see index), a poached egg and Hollandaise sauce.

Special Sunday Eggs

Top toasted English muffins with a fresh tomato slice, a poached egg and crab sauce for crepes (see index).

Spinach Quiche

1 unbaked 9 inch pie shell for quiche
3 tbsp. chopped onion
4 mushrooms, cut in half and sliced
1½ tbsp. butter
¾ cup cooked, well drained spinach (not packed)
4 eggs
1 cup cream
½ cup milk
pinch or two of nutmeg
¼ tsp. salt
½ cup grated Swiss cheese
1½ tbsp. butter

Melt butter in a skillet. Sauté onions and mushrooms. Add spinach, stir with a fork to break up. Cook quickly until liquid is gone. Cool.

Beat eggs well with a wire whisk. Add cream, milk, salt and nutmeg and mix. Stir in spinach mixture with a fork so that is is evenly distributed through the egg/cream mixture. Pour into pie shell, sprinkle with cheese. Cut 1½ tbsp. butter into pea sized pieces and dot top of cheese with it. Bake at 375° for 30 to 35 minutes until a silver knife comes out clean.

Crab Quiche

1 unbaked 9 inch pie shell for quiche
3 tbsp. chopped onion
5 to 6 mushrooms, sliced
3 tbsp. butter
6 oz. crab meat
salt and pepper
3 eggs
1 cup cream
½ cup grated Swiss cheese
1½ tbsp. butter cut into pea sized pieces

Sauté onions and mushrooms in 3 tbsp. butter. Add crab meat, salt and pepper. Raise heat and boil for 1 minute until liquid is gone. Cool.

Beat eggs, add cream and blend. Fold in crab mixture and pour into pie shell. Sprinkle cheese on top, dot with pea sized butter. Bake 30 minutes at 375°. Serve hot or cold.

Pie Crust for Quiche

¾ cup unbleached white flour
¼ tsp. salt
4 tbsp. butter
2 tbsp. ice water

Sift salt and flour together. Cut butter into flour with pastry blender or fork until crumbly. Add ice water and stir with fork until it forms a ball. Chill for 1 hour before rolling out on lightly floured board. Makes a single 9 inch crust.

Crepes

3 eggs
1 cup flour
¼ tsp. salt
1 cup milk
¼ cup water
2 tsp. melted butter

Beat eggs until light. Add sifted flour and salt, beat until smooth. Gradually add milk and water, beating until well blended. Add melted butter and stir.

Pour 2 tbsp. of the batter (a large measuring cup is ideal to use) into a lightly buttered 8 inch crepe pan. Tilt pan and pour batter into center, turning pan from side to side until batter covers bottom of pan. When one side of the crepe is browned (about 1 minute), turn over and brown the other side. The first side is the "good" side that is folded to the outside when used.

Crepes may be made ahead and stored in a plastic bag or frozen. When stacking them put paper doilies between each one. The doilies can be reused. Makes 12 to 14 crepes.

Crab Crepes

4 tbsp. butter
2 tbsp. minced onion
3 tbsp. flour
1¼ cups milk
1 cup cream
salt and pepper to taste
4 tbsp. dry sherry
10 mushrooms, sliced
2 tbsp. butter
½ lb. crab meat
10 crepes

Melt 4 tbsp. butter in a saucepan. Sauté onions. Stir in flour and cook 2 to 3 minutes on medium heat, stirring with a wire whisk. Add milk and cream and cook, stirring, until thickened and bubbly. Stir in sherry.

Sauté mushrooms in another pan in 2 tbsp. butter. Add crab and heat for 1 to 2 minutes. Add mushrooms and crab to cream sauce, blend.

Place 2 tbsp. crab mixture in center of each crepe and roll up, placing them seam side down in a buttered shallow baking pan. Pour remaining sauce on top and bake in a 400° oven for 5 to 10 minutes until hot. Makes 10.

Spinach Crepes and Mornay Sauce

2 cups cooked, drained spinach
3 tbsp. chopped onion
3 mushrooms, chopped
1 tbsp. butter
1 tbsp. lemon juice
6 crepes

Melt butter in a skillet, saute onion and mushrooms. Add spinach and lemon juice. Stir well with a fork, cooking until juices are gone. Place spinach mixture in center of each crepe and roll up. Put seam side down in a greased shallow baking dish.

Mornay Sauce

2 tbsp. butter
1 tbsp. flour
2 tsp. very finely minced onion
pinch or two of nutmeg
1 cup milk
¼ tsp. salt
3 tbsp. grated Parmesan cheese
3 tbsp. grated Swiss cheese
1 tbsp. butter

Melt butter in a skillet, sauté onion until limp. Stir in flour and nutmeg, cook 2 to 3 minutes, stirring with a wire whisk. Add milk and salt, cook stirring until thickened and bubbly. Blend in grated cheeses and cook stirring until the cheese melts. Stir in 1 tbsp. butter and blend well. Spoon over crepes in pan. Bake at 400° for 5 to 7 minutes until hot.

Cheese Soufflé

3 tbsp. butter
3 tbsp. flour
1 cup milk
¾ cup grated Cheddar cheese
¼ tsp. Worcestershire sauce
3 eggs, separated (room temperature)
⅛ tsp. cream of tartar

Melt butter in saucepan, blend in flour. Cook stirring for 2 to 3 minutes. Slowly add milk, stirring constantly with a wire whisk. Cook over medium heat, stirring, until thickened. Add cheese and stir until cheese melts. Add salt, pepper and Worcestershire sauce. Put a spoonful of sauce into the slightly beaten egg yolks, stir egg yolks into sauce. (If you put the egg yolks directly into the hot sauce they may curdle.) Cool.

Beat egg whites and cream of tartar until they stand in peaks, stiff but not dry. (If too dry the soufflé will fall.) Fold egg whites into the cheese mixture, pour into greased 1 quart soufflé dish. Bake at 350° for 30 to 35 minutes until soufflé is puffed and brown. Serve immediately. Serve with peach chutney (see index) or peach jam. Serves four.

To make a puff on the top of a soufflé, cut a circle on top with a rubber spatula 1 inch deep and 1½ inches from edge.

Cheese Puff

This has more substance than a cheese soufflé.
Serve for lunch or a light supper with a salad. Try
spiced peaches or peach chutney with it (see index).

8 to 10 slices stale French bread
4 tbsp. soft butter
2 tbsp. prepared mustard
2½ cups grated sharp Cheddar cheese (8 oz.)
½ cup grated Parmesan cheese
3 eggs
3 cups milk
1 tsp. Worcestershire sauce
½ tsp. salt
paprika

Mix mustard and butter together in a small bowl until
well blended. Spread on bread. Cut bread into fourths
(yield: 4 cups). Layer bread in a greased 9" by 9"
baking dish, sprinkle each layer with Cheddar and
Parmesan cheeses.

Beat eggs with Worcestershire sauce and salt, blend in
milk. Pour over bread and cheese and sprinkle lightly
with paprika. Cover and chill several hours or
overnight. Bake uncovered at 350° for 1 hour. Serves
four to six.

Swiss Fondue

1 lb. grated cheese, Jarlsburg or Swiss
   (or half Gruyere)
1½ cups dry white wine
4 tsp. cornstarch mixed with 4 tsp. water
1 clove garlic
2 tbsp. Kirsch

Rub the inside of a pan with cut garlic clove. (You can use a chafing dish, a double boiler, a heavy casserole on an asbestos pad on the stove, or a large heavy pot on low heat. Stir fondue with a wire whisk.) Add wine and heat. Add grated cheese and stir until melted. Add cornstarch and Kirsch and stir until bubbly. Serve with cubes of French bread, to dip into fondue with a fork.

Lasagne

This recipe may be a little longer than others, but is worth the time. It is better made ahead and reheated.

¾ to 1 lb. ricotta cheese
½ lb. lasagne noodles

Meat Sauce
1 large onion, finely chopped
1 clove garlic, finely minced
2 tsp. parsley
4 tbsp. vegetable oil
3½ cups canned pear shaped tomatoes
    (1 lb. 12 oz.)
1 can tomato paste (6 oz.)
1 bay leaf
1 tsp. salt
¾ cup water
¼ cup dry red wine
¾ lb. lean ground meat
¾ lb. Italian sausage

Cheese Sauce
1 small onion, finely chopped
4 tbsp. butter or margarine
3 tbsp. flour
⅓ cup grated Mozarella cheese
⅔ cup grated Parmesan cheese
2 cups milk
2 egg yolks

Cook noodles in boiling, salted water with a little oil added. When tender, drain and cover with cold water to prevent them from sticking.

Meat Sauce

Heat oil in a large pot or Dutch oven, sauté garlic and onion, add parsley, tomatoes, tomato paste, salt, water and wine. Mash tomatoes and stir until well blended. Bring to a boil, crumble in ground beef and sausage (uncooked), cover and let simmer 45 minutes, stirring occasionally, breaking up meat and tomatoes.

Cheese Sauce

Melt butter in a large saucepan, add onion and cook 2 minutes. Mix in flour and a dash of salt, stir until smooth. Add grated cheese. Gradually add milk and cook over low heat, stirring constantly, until cheese has completely melted and sauce is not stringy. Beat egg yolks slightly in a small bowl, add some of the cheese mixture and pour all back into the pan. Cook stirring over low heat for 10 minutes.

Grease a 9" by 12" baking dish, put a layer of noodles in it, spoon ¼ of the ricotta cheese on them. (It is creamy and will not spread evenly, but will blend when cooked.) Next put on ¼ of the meat sauce and ¼ of the cheese sauce, spreading it with the back of a spoon. Repeat for 4 layers, ending with cheese.

Bake at 325° for 20 minutes, let it sit for 4 to 5 hours or overnight in the refrigerator. When ready to serve, heat for 10 to 15 minutes at 325° until hot throughout. Serves eight to ten.

Crab Spaghetti

½ lb. spaghetti
¾ to 1 lb. crab meat
8 mushrooms, sliced
2 tbsp. butter
1 can tomato sauce (8 oz.)
½ cup dry white wine
½ cup water
1 tsp. parsley
½ tsp. sweet basil
¼ tsp. salt
½ lb. Tillamook or mild yellow cheese, grated

Cook and drain spaghetti. Place in buttered casserole. Sauté mushrooms in butter, add crab and cook for 2 minutes. Add tomato sauce, wine, water, spices and one half of grated cheese, blend. Pour sauce on spaghetti and mix thoroughly. Top with remaining cheese and bake for 30 minutes at 350°. Do not overcook. Serves four to six.

Clam Sauce for Spaghetti

2 cloves garlic, finely minced
3 tbsp. olive oil
6 tbsp. butter
1 tbsp. lemon juice
¼ tsp. salt
1 tsp. dried parsley
1 can chopped clams (7 oz.)
1 can button mushrooms (2 oz.)
1 green onion, chopped

Sauté garlic in oil and butter, do not brown. Add parsley, salt and lemon juice, stir and cook over low heat until creamy. Add clams and juice, stir and simmer for 4 to 5 minutes until well blended. Add mushrooms and green onions, cook 1 minute more. Serve over spaghetti, sprinkle with grated Parmesan cheese. Serves two to three and can be easily doubled.

Fettucine

½ lb. fresh thin noodles (see index)
½ cup butter
½ cup cream
½ cup Parmesan cheese
freshly ground black pepper
½ tsp. salt

Cook noodles in boiling water for 4 to 5 minutes. Drain well. Melt butter on low heat. Add cream and blend well with wire whisk. Pour on noodles and toss until noodles are coated. Grind pepper over noodles and toss again. Sprinkle cheese on noodles and toss well until fully blended and creamy.

An alternative method: slightly whip cream in a small bowl. Melt butter over low heat. Stir in cheese and add cream. Whip with wire whisk until light and well blended. Pour over noodles and toss until well mixed.

To make larger or smaller amounts, use equal proportions of cheese, cream and butter.

Curried Meat Loaf

This is an unusual meat loaf; don't be too strict with the spices, you can alter them to fit your taste.

1 onion, chopped
2 green apples, cored, peeled and chopped
2 tbsp. butter
1 to 1½ lbs. lean ground beef
2 slices of bread, soaked in milk to cover
2 eggs
2 tbsp. curry powder
2 tbsp. brown sugar
2 tbsp. apple cider vinegar
2 tbsp. chutney
¼ tsp. salt
¼ tsp. pepper
¼ tsp. each of coriander, cinnamon
　and nutmeg (optional)
½ cup raisins
¼ cup almonds (optional)

In a skillet, sauté onions and apples in butter until clear and soft. Transfer to a large mixing bowl and add all other ingredients. Mix well with a fork until ingredients are thoroughly combined. Bake in loaf pan at 350° for 1 hour to 1 hour and 15 minutes. Serves four to six.

Chili

5 cloves garlic, minced
3 medium onions, thickly sliced
¼ cup olive oil
2 cans red kidney beans, drained
    (1 lb. 13 oz. each)
2 cans pear shaped tomatoes
    (1 lb. 12 oz. each)
1 pint beer
1 can tomato puree (15 oz.)
1 can tomato paste (12 oz.)
1 can tomato paste (6 oz.)
½ bay leaf
½ cup molasses
4 tbsp. chili powder
1 tsp. oregano
1 tsp. dry mustard
4 tbsp. instant coffee
1 tsp. nutmeg
hot sauce to taste
salt to taste
dash of nutmeg
1 lb. lean ground beef
1 lb. hot sausage
1 can pitted medium size ripe olives (6 oz.)

Cook onions and garlic in olive oil for 15 minutes, stirring occasionally. Add all remaining ingredients except olives and meat. Cook over low heat for at least 8 hours.

Half an hour before serving, cook sausage, drain and add to sauce. Cook hamburger in big chunks and add to sauce. Add drained olives just before serving. Serves eight to ten.

Joe's Special

1 lb. lean ground beef
½ cup chopped onion
6 to 8 mushrooms, sliced
2 tsp. olive oil
1 tbsp. butter
1 cup cooked, chopped broccoli or spinach
4 eggs, beaten

Sauté onions and mushrooms in oil and butter in a large, heavy skillet. Add meat and cook until crumbly. Add vegetables and mix well. Add eggs and stir until eggs are cooked. Serves four.

Hamburgers

Hamburgers are something we seem to think of as a fast food or a "last resort." Here are five kinds that with a Caesar salad or baked beans (see index) make a satisfying meal. Use a good grade of ground beef and either barbeque them or cook them in a hot preheated skillet on both sides (to seal in the juices). Then turn down the heat, and cook to the desired degree of doneness.

Barbequed Hamburgers

1 cup chili sauce (see index)
⅓ tsp. chili powder
3 tbsp. olive oil
2 tbsp. lemon juice
1 tsp. brown sugar
2 tsp. tarragon vinegar
⅓ bay leaf
1 tsp. Tabasco sauce
2 tbsp. water
⅔ cup chopped onion
1 clove garlic, minced
½ tsp. salt

Combine all ingredients in a saucepan, bring to a boil and simmer, stirring occasionally for 15 minutes. Cool. Use ⅓ cup per pound of ground meat, mix thoroughly. These are best barbequed. The sauce will keep in the refrigerator.

Special Hamburgers

Thinly slice red onion and mushrooms (two slices onion and 1 to 2 mushrooms for each hamburger). Sauté in butter and serve on top of cooked hamburger. Butter buns and either grill them in skillet or toast lightly under broiler.

Patty Melt Cheeseburgers

Shape ground meat to fit into rye bread. Cook hamburgers and top with a slice of Cheddar cheese when done. Cover until cheese melts. In a separate pan, sauté thinly sliced white onion in butter. Place on hamburger. Grill buttered rye bread in pan used for onions. Place hamburger on ungrilled side of bread.

Guacamole Hamburgers

Top cooked hamburgers with a slice of tomato, onion and guacamole (see index).

Pepper Hamburgers

Shape hamburger to fit on sliced sour dough or French bread. Sprinkle both sides with coarse ground black pepper and press in. Cook. Butter one side of bread and grill to golden brown in heavy skillet. Place hamburger on ungrilled side of bread.

Green Chili Enchiladas

2 to 2½ cups cooked, diced chicken
½ cup chopped onion
½ to ⅔ cup grated Monterey Jack cheese
8 tortillas
oil for frying tortillas
green chili enchilada sauce

Mix chicken, onion and cheese in medium sized bowl. Fry tortillas in oil until soft, not crisp. Dip in warm enchilada sauce, stack on plate. Place 2 to 3 tbsp. chicken mixture across center of tortilla and roll up. Put rolled tortillas, flap side down in a greased shallow baking dish. Place close together. Bake for 350° for 20 minutes. Place on plate and spoon heated sauce over them.

Green Chili Enchilada Sauce

½ clove garlic, finely minced
½ cup chopped onion
1 can mild green chili peppers (4 oz.)
2 cans green tomatoes, drained (12 oz. each)
1¼ cups chicken broth
2 tbsp. vegetable oil
½ tsp. salt
½ tsp. sugar

Mix everything together except oil, salt and sugar. Put half in blender and blend. Heat oil in a large skillet, pour sauce into heated oil. Blend other half and pour into pan. Bring to a boil, add salt and sugar, turn to low and simmer, stirring occasionally for 10 to 15 minutes until sauce has thickened. This sauce freezes well.

Chicken Tostadas with Lemon Dressing

For each tostada you need:

½ cup diced, cooked chicken
¼ cup shredded iceburg lettuce
2 slices tomato
3 tbsp. grated Monterey Jack cheese
1 tortilla
oil for frying tortilla

Fry tortilla until crisp, drain on paper towel. Place chicken, tomato, lettuce and cheese on tortilla. Pour lemon dressing on top.

Lemon Dressing

3 tbsp. salad oil
3 tbsp. lemon juice
¼ tsp. salt

Combine in a small jar and shake until creamy. This is enough for four tostadas. To make a larger amount use lemon juice and oil in equal proportions.

Chicken Tacitos

Left over turkey may also be used.

2 cups cooked, diced chicken
½ to ⅔ cup green chili salsa
8 tortillas
oil for frying tortillas

Mix chicken and salsa. Mixture should not be too moist. Heat oil and cook tortillas quickly on each side. (They should be soft, not crisp.) Stack them on a plate to drain. Place a few tbsp. of chicken mixture across the center and roll up. Place them on a cookie sheet close together with the flap of the tortilla on the bottom. Bake at 350° until crisp. Serve with either sour cream or guacamole (see index).

Green Chili Salsa

¼ cup chopped onion
2 tbsp. vegetable oil
1 can chopped mild green peppers (4 oz.)
1 can whole tomatoes (1 lb.)
¼ tsp. sugar
½ tsp. salt

Sauté onion in oil, add tomatoes (juice and all). Mash with wooden spoon or potato masher. Add chilies, salt and sugar, bring to a boil, turn down heat and simmer for 5 minutes, stirring often, until thickened. If you like a hotter salsa, add a few drops of Tabasco sauce or ground red chili peppers. This sauce will keep refrigerated and also freezes well.

Stuffed Cabbage Rolls

1 head cabbage
¾ lb. lean ground beef
¾ lb. ground pork
1 cup uncooked rice
½ cup finely chopped onion
1 egg
1 tsp. pepper
2 tsp. salt
1 tbsp. paprika
2½ cups tomato juice
3 cups water
1 cup sour cream

Core cabbage and place head down in boiling water to cover. Turn off heat. When cabbage has wilted, remove from water and peel leaves off, leaving them whole.

Combine meat, onion, egg, seasonings and rice. Mix well. In the center of each cabbage leaf, place 2 to 3 tbsp. of filling. Fold sides in like an envelope and roll up.

Place in Dutch oven or in large kettle and cover with water and tomato juice. Bring to a boil, turn heat down and simmer covered for 1½ hours. Place cabbage rolls on serving dish. Mix a little of the liquid with sour cream and pour over rolls. Serves eight.

Spinach Beef Stew

1½ lbs. round steak or stew meat,
   cut into small pieces
2 tbsp. vegetable oil
3 medium tomatoes
1 tsp. salt
1½ cups water
2 large onions, thinly sliced
½ lb. fresh spinach or chard

Brown meat in oil in a large Dutch oven or heavy pot. Chop one tomato and add to meat with water and salt. Stir and cover. Cook simmering until meat is tender; 45 minutes to 1½ hours depending on the cut of meat.

Slice two tomatoes. Place onions, tomatoes and spinach over meat, cover and cook over medium heat for 15 minutes. Serve over rice. Serves four to six.

Hangtown Fry

2 strips bacon
3 medium oysters, drained
1 tbsp. flour
pinch of salt
¼ cup dry bread crumbs
2 eggs
½ tsp. water
¼ tsp. chives
pinch of salt

Cook bacon until crisp in a small skillet or omelet pan. Drain on paper towel and set aside.

Put flour and salt into a small paper bag, toss oysters until coated. (The oysters may be cut in half.)

Beat eggs with water and a pinch of salt in a small bowl. Dip floured oysters into eggs, roll in bread crumbs. Fry until browned in bacon grease; 2 to 3 minutes on each side. Add chives to eggs and pour over oysters. Cook without stirring (like an omelet, but do not fold) until eggs are set. A cover at this point will help the eggs to set. Top with crisp bacon and serve.

French fried potatoes make a nice side dish. Fresh lemon juice may be squeezed over the omelet if desired. Serves one.

Chicken and Asparagus Casserole

2 cups cooked chicken breasts, cut up
1½ cups cooked asparagus, cut up
6 to 8 mushrooms, sliced
2 tbsp. butter or margarine
1 can cream of asparagus soup
1⅓ cups quick cooking rice
1½ cups boiling water

Sauté mushrooms in butter. Put into buttered casserole. Add chicken, asparagus, rice and soup, mix well. Stir in 1½ cups boiling water, stir again. Bake covered at 400° for 15 minutes. Serves four to six.

ENTREES

ENTREES

ENTREES

ENTREES

ENTREES

ENTREES

Pepper Steak

small fillet of beef 1 to 1¼ inches thick (per person)
freshly ground black pepper
2 tbsp. butter
few drops of oil
½ cup dry white wine
1 tbsp. brandy
2 tsp. butter

Cover both sides of meat with pepper. Press into meat. Heat oil and butter in heavy skillet and sear steak on both sides. Continue cooking until meat is the way you like it. Remove to platter. Stir wine and brandy into pan juices, bring to a boil. Turn heat down and cook until reduced by ¼; 5 to 10 minutes, stirring constantly. Add 2 tsp. butter, stir quickly and pour over steak.

Medallions

1 fillet of beef, 1 to 1½ inches thick (per person)
1 day old bread round, eggplant slice or artichoke
    bottom (per person)
egg
butter for frying

Beat egg in a small bowl, season with salt and pepper.
Dip bread round (or eggplant or artichoke bottom)
into egg and fry in butter on both sides until brown.
Remove to warm plate or oven.

Quickly cook steak in a heavy skillet in butter, or
broil it the way you like it. Place steak on bread round
(eggplant, or artichoke bottom) and top with Bearnaise sauce.

Bearnaise Sauce

½ tsp. finely chopped shallots
½ tsp. dried tarragon
¼ tsp. dried parsley
3 tbsp. dry white wine
2 tbsp. tarragon vinegar
2 tbsp. red wine vinegar
⅛ tsp. freshly ground black pepper
⅓ cup butter
1 tsp. lemon juice
½ tsp. water
2 egg yolks

In a small bowl (not metal) whip egg yolks and water with a wire whisk until thick and lemon colored; 1 to 2 minutes. Put spices, wine and vinegar in a small saucepan (not aluminum), bring to a boil, and boil until reduced by ⅓; 5 to 7 minutes. Remove from heat and stir in butter, put back on low heat until butter melts stirring once or twice. Add lemon juice, heat until it starts to boil, remove from heat. Whip in beaten egg yolks with a wire whisk just until the sauce thickens. (This happens quickly. Do not over beat or it will get too thick.) Serve at once. Makes ½ to ⅔ of a cup.

Stuffed Flank Steak

This can be eaten cold, sliced very thin.
You can serve it as an appetizer, or take it on a picnic
with Muenster cheese and cherry tomatoes,
or marinated artichokes.

1½ lbs. flank steak
2 cups fresh bread crumbs
¼ tsp. sage
2 tsp. parsley
¼ tsp. salt
2 to 3 mushrooms, finely chopped
⅓ to ½ cup chopped onion
4 tbsp. butter or margarine
few drops of oil
2 tbsp. butter or margarine
1 can consommé
1 cup dry red wine

Mix sage, parsley and salt with bread crumbs. Chop
mushrooms and onions, and sauté in 4 tbsp. butter.
Mix into bread crumbs.

Cut off any fat from flank steak. Score diagonally
both ways on both sides, being careful not to cut
through the steak. With your hands form a roll of
dressing down the center of the steak. Roll up and tie
with a string. (If necessary, fasten ends with tooth-
picks so dressing will not come out.)

Heat a few drops of oil in a heavy skillet or Dutch oven. Add butter. Brown steak well on all sides. Pour consommé and wine over steak and bring to a boil. Reduce heat, cover and simmer for 45 minutes to 1 hour or until meat is tender. Turn meat occasionally, basting top with sauce. Remove steak and cook remaining sauce until thick. Pour over steak.

Steak Burgundy

1 fillet of beef 1 to 1¼ inches thick (per person)
2 tbsp. butter
few drops of oil
4 mushrooms, sliced
2 tbsp. butter
½ cup Burgundy wine
1 tbsp. butter

Sauté mushrooms in 2 tbsp. butter. Set aside. Heat oil and 2 tbsp. butter in heavy skillet, sear meat on both sides, cook the way you like it. Remove to plates, top with mushrooms. Pour wine into pan juices and deglaze by stirring with a wire whisk. Bring to a boil and cook until reduced by ¼; 5 to 10 minutes. Whisk 1 tbsp. butter into sauce and pour over steaks.

Beef Bourguignon

2½ lbs. boneless beef chuck or round steak
   cut into 1 to 1½ inch cubes
4 tbsp. butter
1½ tbsp. flour
1 tsp. salt
2 cloves garlic, crushed
2 tbsp. fresh parsley
1 tbsp. chives
2 tbsp. tomato paste
2 cups Burgundy wine
2 cups consommé
1 bay leaf
24 small pearl onions
1½ cups sliced mushrooms

Heat butter in a large Dutch oven, quickly brown the meat on all sides. (Brown as much as will fit in the pan, then remove and repeat until all of the meat is done and return to pot.) Sprinkle flour over beef and mix well. Add salt, garlic, parsley, chives, tomato paste, bay leaf, wine and consommé, mix well. Cover and simmer for 45 minutes. Mix in onions and mushrooms, cover and simmer for 45 minutes to 1 hour, until beef is tender. Serve with fresh noodles (see index). Serves four to six.

If preferred, the meat may be browned in a skillet and transferred to a large casserole and baked in the oven at 350.°

Beef Stroganoff
Don't be alarmed; this stroganoff has a richer, thicker sauce than many.

1½ to 2 lbs. round steak cut into small cubes
2 to 3 tbsp. vegetable oil
4 tbsp. flour
¼ tsp. paprika
¼ tsp. garlic salt
10 to 12 mushrooms, sliced
1 small onion, chopped
2 tbsp. butter
1 can consommé
¼ cup dry sherry (optional)
½ bay leaf
1 tsp. Worcestershire sauce
½ pint sour cream

Put flour, paprika and garlic salt in a small paper bag. Add steak and shake to coat. Heat oil in a heavy skillet and quickly brown the meat. Add consommé, bay leaf, Worcestershire sauce and sherry (if used). Cover and simmer until meat is tender, stirring occasionally; 20 to 25 minutes.

Sauté onions and mushrooms in butter and add to the meat for the last 5 to 10 minutes. Stir in sour cream (do not cook). Serve over rice or noodles (see index). Serves four to six.

Mexican Steak (to barbeque)

top round steak cut 1½ to 1¾ inches thick
1 cup green chili salsa
¼ head iceburg lettuce, finely shredded
½ onion, finely chopped
1 tomato, finely chopped
1 cup grated Monterey Jack cheese
12 flour tortillas

Marinate steak in 1 cup of salsa for 2 hours, piercing meat with a fork and turning once or twice. Barbeque over hot coals, until medium rare, basting with salsa.

Mix lettuce, onion, tomato, and cheese in a large bowl. Warm flour tortillas. (They can be wrapped in foil and put on one side of the grill while cooking meat.) Cut steak diagonally in very thin slices. Place several slices of steak in a tortilla, spoon in several tablespoons of lettuce mixture and roll up. Serve extra salsa in a bowl. Serves six.

Green Chili Salsa:

¼ cup chopped onion
2 tbsp. vegetable oil
1 can chopped mild green chili peppers (4 oz.)
1 can whole tomatoes (1 lb.)
½ tsp. sugar
½ tsp. salt

Sauté onion in oil. Add tomatoes, juice and all. Mash with a wooden spoon. Add chilies, salt and sugar and bring to a boil. Turn heat down and simmer for 5 minutes until thickened. If you prefer a hotter salsa, add a little chili pepper.

Oyster Beef

This recipe uses oyster sauce which keeps indefinitely in the refrigerator. It can be made without it.

1½ lbs. top round steak
2 tsp. oil
¼ cup soy sauce
¼ cup pale dry sherry
1 clove garlic, finely minced
2 thin slices ginger root, minced
2 tbsp. oyster sauce
enough water to equal 1 cup
2 tsp. cornstarch mixed with 2 tsp. water

Mix soy sauce, sherry, garlic, ginger, and oyster sauce together, add enough water to measure 1 cup.

Cut steak in half lengthwise, then in thin strips across the grain. Heat oil very hot in heavy skillet (or wok) and quickly cook the meat until almost done.

Add sauce to the meat and stir. Bring to boil. Stir in cornstarch mixture and bring to boil stirring until thickened; 2 to 4 minutes. Serve over rice. Serves four.

¾ cup cooked broccoli can be added to this.

Sauerbraten
(German Pot Roast)

3 to 4 lbs. beef rump roast
3 cups apple cider vinegar
3 cups water
2 onions, thinly sliced
4 tbsp. sugar
1 tsp. whole peppercorns
1 tsp. salt
2 bay leaves
½ to 1 tsp. ground ginger
½ lemon, sliced very thin
4 tbsp. bacon drippings
3 tbsp. flour

Put everything but the roast, bacon drippings and flour in a large saucepan and bring to a boil. Place roast in earthenware crock or bowl or enamel pot. (Do not put in metal.) Pour boiling mixture over roast, put cover on and let stand 2 to 5 days, turning meat daily. This can be kept refrigerated for a week. The longer it stands, the sharper it gets.

In a Dutch oven, brown the roast well on all sides in hot bacon drippings. Strain the marinade and add to roast, cover and cook like a pot roast for 2 hours or until meat is tender. Remove meat and thicken gravy with flour which has been mixed with cold water to make a thin mixture. Serve with potato pancakes and red cabbage (see index).

Veal Oscar

½ lb. veal, thinly sliced
flour
1 to 2 tbsp. butter
few drops of oil
2 tbsp. consommé
¼ lb. crab meat or 2 crab legs
1 tbsp. butter
4 to 6 cooked asparagus stalks
Bearnaise sauce

Place veal between two sheets of butcher paper and pound with a wooden mallet or rolling pin until thin. (Sometimes the butcher will do this for you.) Dredge veal in flour to coat both sides. Heat butter and oil until foamy in heavy skillet and brown veal on both sides. Remove to warm plate or oven. Add consommé to pan, turn up heat and cook stirring until liquid is reduced and sauce is thick.

In a small frying pan, sauté crab in 1 tbsp. butter. Pour sauce over veal, top with crab, place asparagus on top of crab and pour Bearnaise sauce over all. Serves two.

Bearnaise Sauce

½ tsp. finely chopped shallots
½ tsp. dried tarragon
¼ tsp. dried parsley
3 tbsp. dry white wine
2 tbsp. tarragon vinegar
2 tbsp. red wine vinegar
⅛ tsp. freshly ground black pepper
⅓ cup butter
1 tsp. lemon juice
½ tsp. water
2 egg yolks

In a small bowl (not metal) whip egg yolks and water with a wire whisk until thick and lemon colored; 1 to 2 minutes. Put spices, wine and vinegar in a small saucepan (not aluminum), bring to a boil and boil until reduced by ⅓; 5 to 7 minutes. Remove from heat and stir in butter, put back on low heat until butter melts, stirring once or twice. Add lemon juice, heat until it starts to boil, remove from heat. Whip in beaten egg yolks with a wire whisk just until sauce thickens. (This happens quickly, do not over beat it, or it will get too thick.) Serve at once. Makes ½ to ⅔ of a cup.

Veal Marsala

1½ lbs. thin veal
4 tbsp. butter
flour
½ clove garlic, finely minced
3 green onions, finely chopped
½ lb. mushrooms, sliced
1 to 2 tbsp. butter
¾ to 1 cup Marsala wine
½ tsp. parsley
salt and pepper to taste

Cut veal into dollar sized pieces and pound until very thin. (Put veal between butcher paper and pound with a wooden mallet or rolling pin, or have the butcher do this.)

Sauté onion, mushrooms and garlic in 3 tbsp. butter. Set aside.

Dredge veal in flour. Heat 4 tbsp. butter with a few drops of oil to prevent burning and quickly brown the veal on both sides. Add mushrooms and onions and stir. Add wine and parsley, stir and simmer until veal is tender and sauce is thickened; 5 to 8 minutes. Serves four.

Scalloped Veal

1½ lbs. boneless veal
1 well beaten egg
½ cup bread crumbs
½ tsp. salt
4 tbsp. oil
½ to ¾ cup milk

Cut veal into ¾ inch cubes. Beat egg until very light in a bowl. Mix bread crumbs and salt together on a plate. Dip veal into egg and roll in bread crumbs. Heat oil in heavy skillet and brown the veal well on all sides. Remove to buttered casserole. This can be done ahead.

Pour milk over veal (enough to cover most of the veal but barely to the top layer). Cover and bake at 350° for 1 to 1½ hours until milk is gone and veal is tender. Serves four.

Roast Lamb with Garlic and Pepper

half or whole leg of lamb
salad oil
coarsely ground black pepper
1 to 2 cloves garlic

Preheat oven to 400.° Peel and cut garlic into thirds, pierce lamb with knife and insert garlic into meaty parts of roast. Brush oil over outside of lamb, sprinkle with black pepper. Place on rack and roast uncovered at 400° for 15 minutes. Turn oven down to 325° and roast 15 to 20 minutes per pound.

Boned (Butterflied) Leg of Lamb

This simple and elegant dish can be served with any kind of vegetable and takes very little time to prepare.

Have your butcher bone a leg of lamb, and remove as much fat as possible.

With Creme de Menthe

leg of lamb, boned
¼ to ½ cup creme de menthe
salt and pepper to taste

Put lamb in baking dish. Pour creme de menthe on one side and roll up. Refrigerate overnite, basting several times. Remove from refrigerator one hour before cooking. Season with salt and pepper. Sear at 400° for 10 to 15 minutes, then turn oven down to 325° to 350° and cook for 15 to 20 minutes per pound.

To create other flavors

Pour a little marinade or lemon juice on the meat, or push a few cloves of garlic into it. If you like it plain, merely put it in the oven as is. Follow cooking directions above.

Orange Pork

2 to 2½ lbs. boneless pork tenderloin
¼ cup sugar
1 tsp. white wine vinegar
2 tbsp. lemon juice
½ cup orange juice
grated rind of one orange
2 tbsp. Cointreau or other orange liqueur
½ bouillon cube
¾ cup water
⅓ cup dry white wine
1 tbsp. brandy
2 tsp. cornstarch dissolved in 2 tsp. water

Roast the pork at 400° for 10 minutes. Turn heat down to 350° and roast for 30 to 35 minutes per pound. When done, glaze with orange sauce. Serve any remaining sauce in a small bowl.

Orange Sauce
This can be made ahead up to the point of putting in the cornstarch.

In a heavy skillet caramelize sugar by heating and stirring constantly with a wooden spoon until it melts. It will turn light brown. Remove from heat and add vinegar. (If it gets stiff at this point, do not worry. Cooking will dissolve it.)

Add lemon and orange juices, rind and Cointreau. Put sauce back on heat and bring to a boil. Reduce by ⅓; 5 to 7 minutes. Set aside.

In another saucepan combine bouillon cube, water and wine. Bring to a boil. Cook for 5 minutes. Add orange sauce and brandy and cook simmering for 5 to 7 minutes, until well blended.

Just before serving, bring the sauce to a boil. Add cornstarch mixture and cook stirring until thick and clear. Serves four to six.

Chinese Barbequed Pork

2 lbs. boneless pork tenderloin
marinade
2 tbsp. chicken stock
2 tbsp. soy sauce
1 tbsp. pale dry sherry
1½ tbsp. sugar
¾ tsp. salt
1 tsp. finely minced garlic
1 thin slice ginger root, finely minced
1 green onion (white only), finely minced

Basting Sauce

1 tsp. sugar
1 tbsp. honey
1 tbsp. oil
1 tbsp. catsup

Mix the marinade ingredients together. Cut pork in strips 2 inches thick. Marinate 4 to 5 hours, turning once.

Combine basting sauce ingredients and blend. Roast the pork at 350° for 45 minutes to 1 hour. Turn oven up to 450°, baste meat with basting sauce and roast for 10 minutes more. Turn, baste other side and roast for 10 minutes until golden and cooked through. Slice thin and serve (hot or cold) or use in fried rice.

Barbequed Spareribs

3 to 4 lbs. spareribs
½ onion, finely chopped
½ tsp. salt
½ tsp. chili powder
2 tbsp. brown sugar
2 tbsp. vinegar
2 tbsp. Worcestershire sauce
2 tbsp. crushed pineapple
½ cup catsup
1 cup water

Place spareribs meat side up in shallow roasting pan. Roast at 375° for 30 minutes. Pour off fat, turn down to 350° and roast for 30 minutes more.

In the meantime, combine all other ingredients in a saucepan, bring to a boil, turn to low and simmer for 5 minutes. Pour on spareribs and bake for another 30 to 45 minutes until ribs are tender, turning several times and basting with sauce. (These can be cooked on an outside grill.) Ribs can be placed on a rack over a pan of water. This keeps them moist and prevents grease from spattering. Serves four.

Chinese Barbequed Spareribs

2 lbs. spareribs (have butcher cut ribs in half)
¼ cup soy sauce
2 tbsp. honey
2 tbsp. white vinegar
1 tbsp. dry sherry
1 clove garlic, finely chopped
1 tsp. sugar
2 tbsp. chicken stock

Put spareribs in long shallow glass pan (metal will not do). Combine all ingredients and mix well. Pour sauce over ribs and marinate for 3 to 6 hours, turning occasionally and basting. Place ribs on rack over a pan of water. Roast at 375° for 1 hour. Add water if needed. Turn heat to 450° and roast for 10 minutes, turn ribs and roast 10 minutes more. Cut into individual ribs and serve with plum sauce (see index).

Easy Plum Sauce

1 jar red plum jam
½ tsp. ground ginger
½ tsp. dry mustard
½ tsp. ground lemon peel
1 tbsp. honey
¼ cup apple cider vinegar
1 tsp. minced onion
1 tbsp. minced canned green chili pepper
1 tsp. salt

Combine all ingredients in a saucepan, bring to boil over medium heat. Turn to low and simmer for 15 minutes, stirring. Cool and put in jar. Refrigerate. This will keep indefinitely and is good as a glaze for chicken.

Spareribs and Sauerkraut

1 to 1½ lbs. spareribs
1 can sauerkraut (1 lb.)
2 tbsp. oil
¼ cup chopped onion
½ tsp. caraway seed (if sauerkraut does not
   contain any)

Heat oil in heavy skillet until hot. Brown spareribs
well on both sides. Put undrained sauerkraut on top
of ribs and sprinkle with onion and caraway seed.
Cover and simmer over low heat until spareribs are
tender; about 1 hour. Stir occasionally so juices blend
well. Add more liquid while cooking if needed. Serves
two.

MEAT

MEAT

MEAT

MEAT

MEAT

MEAT

chicken

Chicken Veronique

8 half chicken breasts
8 mushrooms, sliced
4 to 6 tbsp. butter
2 tbsp. flour
1 cup cream
¼ cup dry white wine
⅓ cup diced ham
½ cup white seedless grapes

Brown chicken in skillet in butter. Place in casserole. Sauté mushrooms in the same pan and add to chicken. Add flour to pan juices and stir until smooth. Gradually add cream and wine to pan, blending until smooth. Stir constantly and cook until sauce is thickened. Add diced ham and cook 3 minutes longer. Pour sauce over chicken and mushrooms. Bake covered at 350° for 35 to 40 minutes. Scatter grapes on top and bake uncovered for 10 minutes longer. Serve over rice. Serves four to eight.

Chicken Breasts in White Wine Sauce

8 half chicken breasts
2 green onions, finely chopped
12 mushrooms, thickly sliced
6 tbsp. butter
2 tbsp. flour
1 cup dry white wine
1 cup cream
salt and pepper to taste

Sauté onions and mushrooms in 2 tbsp. butter. Remove from pan and set aside. Add the rest of the butter to pan and brown chicken on both sides until golden brown; 10 to 12 minutes. (If all the chicken cannot be browned at once, do a few pieces at a time.) Remove chicken from pan. Stir flour into pan juices, cook until bubbly. Add wine gradually, cook on medium heat, stirring constantly, until thickened. Slowly add cream and stir until blended. Add mushrooms and onions, blend, add chicken, spooning some of the sauce on top. Cover and simmer 35 to 40 minutes, turning chicken occasionally. Serve over rice. Serves four to eight.

Coq au Vin

2 to 2½ lbs. chicken parts
4 to 6 tbsp. butter
4 tbsp. flour
1 tsp. salt
¼ tsp. pepper
¼ cup brandy
½ slice smoked ham, cut into thin strips
1 clove garlic, crushed
1 bay leaf
½ tsp. parsley
1½ cups Burgundy wine
½ cup consommé
24 small white onions
12 mushrooms, cut in half

Wash and dry chicken. Combine flour, salt and pepper in a paper bag, add chicken and shake until well coated.

In a large Dutch oven melt butter and brown chicken well on all sides. Pour brandy over it, light with a match. When flames are out, add garlic, parsley, bay leaf and ham. Pour in wine and consommé and simmer for 15 minutes. Add mushrooms and onions, simmer covered for 45 minutes or until chicken is tender. Serve with rice. Serves four to six.

Chicken Cacciatore

1 chicken, cut up, or chicken parts
2 tbsp. vegetable oil
2 tbsp. olive oil
¼ cup chopped onion
1 clove garlic, minced
½ cup sliced mushrooms
3½ cups canned tomatoes
½ tsp. sweet basil
¼ tsp. parsley
½ cup dry white wine
½ cup green pepper, seeded and
    cut into strips
1 tsp. salt
¼ cup sliced ripe olives (optional)

Wash chicken and pat dry. Heat vegetable oil in a heavy skillet or Dutch oven, fry chicken until golden brown.

Heat olive oil in another skillet, sauté onion, garlic and mushrooms. Add tomatoes, basil, parsley, salt, wine and green pepper. Bring to a boil, turn down heat and simmer for 20 minutes.

Pour sauce over chicken, add olives if used, cover and simmer until chicken is tender; 35 to 40 minutes. Serve over noodles (see index.) Serves four.

Chicken Tandori (to barbeque)

1½ chickens or chicken parts, cut up
½ cup lemon juice
2 tsp. salt
pinch of saffron (optional)

Marinade

1 cup yogurt
2 cloves garlic, finely minced
1 inch ginger root, peeled and finely chopped
½ tsp. cumin
2 tsp. ground coriander
¼ tsp. red pepper (optional)

Wash and dry chicken. Mix together lemon juice, salt and saffron, brush mixture on chicken pieces, put into large bowl.
Combine marinade ingredients and pour over chicken. Marinate 4 to 5 hours or overnight, turning once or twice, to coat chicken. Barbeque, basting with any remaining sauce. Serves four to six.

Moroccan Chicken

This sounds complicated, but isn't if you do each step in order. The spices combine to make a sweet, mild curry sauce.

1½ chickens cut up or chicken parts for six
2 to 3 tsp. cumin
salt
¾ lb. pitted prunes
2 to 3 tsp. cinnamon
2 large onions, thinly sliced
1 tsp. turmeric
1 tsp. ginger
¼ cup water
1 cup whole or slivered almonds
oil for frying

Wash and dry chicken, sprinkle with salt. Rub cumin on chicken and let sit for 1 hour.

Put prunes and cinnamon in pan, add water to cover prunes. Cook simmering, for 30 minutes.

Put onions in large pot or Dutch oven with turmeric, ginger and water. Steam covered for 15 minutes.

Fry almonds in oil until light brown. Stir over medium heat. Watch carefully, they brown quickly. Drain on paper towel.

Fry chicken in same oil until golden brown, place in pot with onions. Add 1 cup water, cover and simmer 30 minutes. Add prunes and prune water, stir and continue cooking 10 to 15 minutes until chicken is done. Serve over rice and top with almonds. Serves six.

Chicken Heung

3 to 4 chicken breasts, cooked and
   cut into large pieces
4 green onions, minced (white part only)
½ cup sliced mushrooms
2 tbsp. butter
1 cup sour cream
1 tsp. ginger root, minced
⅛ tsp. nutmeg
2 tsp. grated lemon peel
½ cup water chestnuts, sliced
½ cup slivered almonds
¼ tsp. salt

Sauté mushrooms and onions in butter. Add sour cream, stir until well blended. Add ginger, nutmeg, lemon peel and salt. To blended sauce, add water chestnuts and almonds. Pour over chicken in casserole, cover and bake at 350° for 30 to 40 minutes. Serves four to six.

Chicken Curry

Do not cook curry in an iron skillet because it will discolor.

4 tbsp. butter
1 medium onion, chopped
2 tbsp. curry powder (see index)
2 green apples, peeled, cored and chopped
1 cup apple juice
2 cups chicken stock
⅓ cup raisins
10 mushrooms, sliced
2 tbsp. butter
3 whole chicken breasts cooked, boned and cut into chunks

Always cook meat to be used by placing in boiling water. (Start with cold water only when making stock.)

Sauté onions in 4 tbsp. butter in a large skillet or Dutch oven. Add curry powder and cook stirring for several minutes. (This is important: curry powder cannot be added after the liquid. To add more later, cook it in butter first.) Add apple and apple juice, simmer covered, stirring occasionally for 8 to 10 minutes. Mash apples well with a potato masher. Add raisins, chicken stock and salt. Simmer uncovered for 20 minutes stirring frequently.

Sauté mushrooms in 2 tbsp. butter, add chicken and mushrooms to sauce. Simmer covered for 10 to 20 minutes. Serve over rice. Serves four to six.

Condiments for curry

sour cream or yogurt
chopped green onion
grated hard boiled egg
sunflower seeds (see index) or chopped peanuts
chopped fresh tomato
shredded coconut
bacon
chutney (see index)

Lemon Chicken

4 half chicken breasts
2 tbsp. vegetable oil
1 clove garlic, minced
1 medium onion, sliced paper thin
2 tbsp. vegetable oil
2 tbsp. olive oil
6 tbsp. lemon juice
½ cup dry white wine
½ tsp. parsley
1 tsp. grated lemon rind
¼ tsp. salt

Brown chicken well in 2 tbsp. oil in a heavy skillet. Remove to Dutch oven or heavy pot. Sauté garlic and onion in pan juices; 2 to 3 minutes. Do not brown. Add vegetable and olive oils, lemon juice, wine and spices. Blend well, pour over chicken and simmer covered until chicken is done; 30 to 40 minutes. Turn chicken occasionally to coat with sauce. Serve over rice. Serves two to four.

Picnic Chicken

The paprika is what makes the chicken brown.

8 chicken thighs
¼ cup chopped onion
1 clove garlic, minced
1 cube beef bouillon
1 cup water
4 to 6 tbsp. butter or margarine
¼ cup flour
¼ tsp. paprika
¼ tsp. salt

Combine flour, salt and paprika in a paper bag and shake once or twice. Drop chicken into bag and shake to coat with flour. Sauté garlic and onion in 2 tbsp. butter. Add the remaining 4 tbsp. butter and fry chicken until golden brown.

Dissolve bouillon cube in 1 cup boiling water and pour over chicken. Cover and simmer, turning chicken to prevent from sticking. Cook until tender: 20 to 30 minutes. Remove from pan and chill. Allow 2 pieces per person.

Cold Chicken Salad

2 cups cooked chicken breasts, chopped
1½ cups coarsely chopped celery
1½ cups cooked rice
½ cup slivered toasted almonds
¼ cup capers

Toast almonds on a cookie sheet at 275° until they start to pop and turn brown. Watch carefully or they will burn.

Dressing

½ cup sour cream
1 tsp. salt
1 tsp. curry powder
½ cup French dressing (Girrards)

Put chicken, celery, rice, almonds and capers in a large bowl. Mix well. In another bowl combine sour cream, dressing, salt and curry powder. Pour over chicken mixture, stir and blend. Chill at least 1 hour before serving.

Orange Roast Duck

One 4 to 5 lb. duckling
1 stalk celery
½ onion
1 orange, peeled and quartered

Sauce

6 tbsp. brown sugar
1 tbsp. white wine vinegar
juice of ½ lemon
juice of 1½ oranges
thinly sliced rind of 1½ oranges (no white)
¼ cup Cointreau or other orange liqueur
½ cup hot water
6 tbsp. dry white wine
4 tbsp. sherry
2 tbsp. cornstarch dissolved in 4 tbsp. water

Rinse and dry the duck. Chop onion and celery, mix with orange and place in cavity of duck.

Roast duck on rack in pan at 375° for 25 minutes per pound. Pierce thigh joints so fat will drain, turn duck three or four times to make crisp.

Carmelize sugar by heating it in heavy skillet, stirring constantly until it becomes liquid and golden. Remove from heat, stir in vinegar, lemon and orange juices and rind. Blend well, bring to a boil, cook stirring until volume is reduced by ⅓. Remove from heat and add Cointreau. Set aside.

When duck is done, remove to platter.

Drain fat from pan, swirl pan with ½ cup hot water. Add wine and sherry. Strain sauce into a saucepan, add orange sauce and boil for 10 minutes. Stir cornstarch mixture into sauce while boiling, cook stirring until clear; 5 to 10 minutes.

Glaze duck with sauce, serve remaining sauce in a bowl. Serves four.

CHICKEN

CHICKEN

CHICKEN

CHICKEN

CHICKEN

Sole Marguery

8 small fillets of sole
10 to 12 mushrooms, sliced
2 green onions, finely chopped
¼ lb. crab meat
½ cup tiny cooked shrimp
1 cup dry white wine
1 cup cream
4 tbsp. Hollandaise sauce (see index)

Roll fillets up and place in buttered baking dish. Top with mushrooms, onions, crab and shrimp. Pour wine over all and bake at 400° until fish is tender; 15 minutes.

Strain the liquid into a saucepan, add cream and bring to a boil. Cook stirring with a wire whisk until sauce is reduced by ⅓. Remove from heat and stir in Hollandaise sauce. Pour over fish and bake for 3 to 5 minutes. Serves four.

Sole Mouquin

2 to 2½ lbs. fillet of sole
4 tbsp. butter
5 tbsp. flour
1 cup cream
¾ cup chicken stock
¼ cup dry white wine
½ cup grated Parmesan cheese
½ tsp. grated lemon peel
salt and pepper to taste
3 cups cooked spinach
    (or 3 packages frozen chopped spinach)

Melt butter and stir in flour. Add cream and stock, cook stirring constantly until mixture boils and thickens. Add wine, ¼ cup of cheese, lemon peel, salt and pepper. Mix ½ cup sauce with cooked, chopped spinach and spread on bottom of a greased 9" by 12" baking pan. Put fillets on top of spinach and cover with remaining sauce. Sprinkle with remaining cheese and bake at 375° for 25 minutes. Serves four to six.

Trout or Sole Amandine

2 trout or 2 to 4 sole fillets
2 tbsp. butter
few drops of oil
flour
1 tbsp. butter
2 tbsp. slivered almonds

Dip fish lightly in flour. Heat 2 tbsp. butter in skillet with a few drops of oil to prevent burning. When butter foams, sauté fish on both sides until done. (It will flake easily with a fork.) Remove to platter. Add 1 tbsp. butter to pan and quickly brown almonds, stirring so they don't burn. Pour over fish. Top with 1 tsp. lemon juice and fresh parsley if desired. Serves two.

Poached Fish

1 to 1½ lbs. salmon or trout
1 quart water
2 tbsp. dry white wine
thin slice of onion
2 peppercorns

Bring water, wine, onion and peppercorns to a boil, lower heat and gently simmer fish for 8 to 10 minutes (just below the boiling point). The fish may be poached in a covered glass baking dish at 400° for 20 to 30 minutes, or until fish flakes easily with a fork. Remove to platter and top with either of the following sauces. Serves four.

Herb Hollandaise Sauce

4 tbsp. butter
2 tsp. Dijon style mustard
juice of 1 lemon
2 tsp. fresh parsley (½ tsp. dried)
1 tsp. fresh chives (½ tsp. dried)
salt and pepper to taste
4 egg yolks

Beat egg yolks in a small bowl (not metal) until thick and lemon colored. Put butter, lemon juice and spices in a saucepan (not aluminum) on low heat and stir until butter melts. Stir in egg yolks and whisk with wire whisk just until sauce thickens. Do not overcook. Serve immediately. Makes ¾ cup.

Egg Hollandaise Sauce

4 tbsp. butter
juice of 1 lemon
2 hard boiled eggs, finely chopped or grated
1 slightly beaten whole egg
2 tsp. fresh parsley (1 tsp. dried)

Melt butter in a small saucepan (not aluminum) over low heat, add lemon juice and hard boiled egg. (If using dried parsley, add it now.) Cook, stirring often, at a slow boil for 5 minutes. Add beaten egg, whip and cook over medium heat until thick. Add fresh parsley and blend. Serve immediately. Makes ¾ cup.

Coquilles Saint-Jacques

These are two different tasting sauces. One is a light white wine sauce, the other has sherry and cheese.

1 to 1¼ lbs. scallops
1 cup dry white wine
3 tbsp. butter
½ to ⅔ cup chopped onion
1 tsp. salt
2 tbsp. flour
½ cup cream
½ cup milk
1 tsp. lemon juice
1 egg yolk, slightly beaten
8 to 10 mushrooms, sliced
2 tbsp. butter

Rinse scallops in cold water, (cut them in half if they are large). Poach scallops in a saucepan in barely simmering wine for 5 minutes. Set aside.

In a saucepan melt butter and sauté onion until golden. Add flour and stir well, cook for 1 to 2 minutes. Drain liquid from scallops and stir into flour. Add cream, milk and salt. Cook stirring constantly until thickened. Put some of the sauce into the egg yolk, mix and return to sauce. Stir and cook for 2 minutes.

In a separate skillet, sauté mushrooms in 2 tbsp. butter and add to sauce. Add scallops and wine, mix and put into a buttered casserole or individual shells. Bake at 350° for 10 to 15 minutes. May be served with rice. Serves four.

Coquilles Saint-Jacques

1 to 1¼ lbs. scallops
½ cup dry sherry
6 tbsp. butter
¼ to ⅓ cup chopped onion
4 tbsp. flour
½ cup milk
1 cup cream
½ tsp. salt
1 tsp. Worcestershire sauce (optional)
8 to 10 mushrooms, sliced
2 tbsp. butter
4 tbsp. grated Gruyere cheese

Rinse scallops in cold water, (cut in half if they are large). Put scallops and sherry in a small bowl. Set aside.

Melt butter in a saucepan, sauté onion until golden. Stir in flour and cook for 1 to 2 minutes. Add cream, milk, salt and Worcestershire sauce and cook over medium heat, stirring constantly, until thickened. Add grated cheese and stir until cheese is melted.

Sauté mushrooms in a skillet in 2 tbsp. butter, add to sauce. Stir in scallops and sherry, mix well, cook 1 to 2 minutes. Pour into buttered casserole or individual shells, bake at 350° for 20 minutes. May be served with rice. Serves four.

Scampi

2 lbs. medium shrimp, shelled and cleaned*
1 cup chopped onion
3 to 5 cloves garlic, minced
½ tsp. salt
1 tbsp. parsley
1 cup butter
½ cup olive oil
5 tbsp. lemon juice
¼ cup dry white wine

Sauté garlic in ¼ cup oil. Do not brown. Add ¼ cup butter and melt. Sauté onion in butter/oil mixture until limp. Add remaining oil and butter, stir until butter melts. Add parsley, salt, lemon juice and wine. Simmer, stirring occasionally until sauce is blended and creamy; 5 to 10 minutes. Add shrimp and cook on low heat, covered, until shrimp turns pink: 3 to 5 minutes. Do not boil or use high heat, or shrimp will get tough. Serve with unseasoned cooked spinach and French bread. Serves four to six.

*To clean shrimp: rinse in cold water, pull off shells and with a sharp knife, cut down back and remove dark vein. Slightly slice the inner curve of the shrimp.

Chinese Fried Shrimp

½ lb. medium shrimp (about 24 shrimp)

Pull shells from shrimp, but leave the tails on them. Rinse well in cold water, drain.

Batter

⅓ cup tapioca
½ cup flour
1 tsp. baking powder
1 tsp. salt
1 egg, beaten
½ cup water

Put tapioca, flour, baking powder and salt in a bowl. Add water and egg and beat with a wire whisk to make a thick batter. If necessary add more water. Let batter stand for ½ hour.

Dip shrimp in batter to coat, let any excess drip off. Deep fry in hot (350°) oil, turn when golden brown. Keep warm in the oven until ready to serve. Serve with hot mustard and catsup.

Cioppino

4 tbsp. olive oil
1 to 2 cloves garlic, finely minced
1¼ cups chopped onion
2 tsp. parsley
2 to 3 tsp. sweet basil
3 cans pear shaped tomatoes (1 lb. 12 oz.)
½ tsp. salt
6 tbsp. dry red wine
1 whole crab or ½ to ¾ lb. crab meat
1 lb. shrimp
1 lb. clams
1½ lbs. turbot or other mild white fish

Sauté garlic and onion in oil in a heavy pot or Dutch oven. Add parsley and sweet basil and stir quickly. Add tomatoes, salt and wine. Mash tomatoes to break apart.

Bring sauce to a boil, turn down to low and simmer for 45 minutes, stirring occasionally.

Put shrimp in boiling water. Cook for 2 minutes or just until they turn pink. Drain and cool. Remove shells. Scrub clams well in cold water and set aside. Remove meat from crab.

Add turbot to tomatoes and cook slowly until tender: about 20 minutes. Break turbot into small pieces with a fork. Add crab, shrimp, and clams and cook 10 to 12 minutes or until clams open. Stir well. Serve in bowls. Serves six to eight.

Crab and Oysters

6 to 8 mushrooms, sliced
¼ cup chopped onion
3 tbsp. butter
1 jar oysters (10 oz.)
½ lb. crab meat
½ cup dry white wine
¾ to 1 cup grated Tillamook cheese

Melt butter in a skillet, sauté onions and mushrooms, remove to a buttered casserole. Put oysters and their liquid into skillet, heat just until the edges curl. Cut into bite sized pieces and pour all into casserole. Add crab meat, salt and pepper and stir. Pour wine over all and top with cheese. Bake at 375° until bubbly and cheese is melted; 15 to 20 minutes. Serves four.

Barbequed Fish

2 lbs. swordfish or red snapper
⅔ cup butter
6 tbsp. lemon juice

Melt butter, add lemon juice and blend well. Brush on fish and grill over charcoal, brushing more sauce on fish while cooking.

Lemon Herb Butter for Fish

⅓ cup butter
2 tbsp. lemon juice
¼ tsp. parsley
¼ tsp. chives
salt

Melt butter, add lemon juice and spices, blend well. Serve over broiled mild white fish.

FISH

FISH

Creamed Spinach with Sour Cream

1 tbsp. oil
3 tbsp. butter
2 cloves garlic, minced
1 onion, finely chopped
3 cups cooked, drained, chopped spinach
1 tsp. nutmeg
6 tbsp. sour cream
salt and pepper to taste

In a large frying pan, heat butter and oil. When frothy, add garlic and onion and cook until clear. Add spinach and mix thoroughly until spinach and onions are combined. Add nutmeg and sour cream and mix again, until all ingredients are combined. Salt and pepper to taste. Spinach needs a lot of salt, so don't be shy. Serves four to six.

Spinach or Broccoli Soufflé

3 tbsp. butter
3 tbsp. flour
1 cup milk
1 cup cooked, chopped, spinach or
    broccoli (well drained)
1 to 2 tsp. lemon juice (optional)
salt and pepper
3 eggs, separated (room temperature)
$1/_8$ tsp. cream of tartar

Egg whites gain more volume if they are beaten at room temperature with cream of tartar.

Melt butter in saucepan and blend in flour with wire whisk. Cook stirring until golden; 2 to 3 minutes. Slowly add milk and cook over medium heat, stirring until thickened. Put a spoonful of sauce into egg yolks and stir egg yolks into sauce. (If you put the egg yolks directly into the hot sauce they may curdle.) Stir in spinach. Cool.

Beat egg whites and cream of tartar until they stand in peaks; stiff but not dry. (Otherwise the soufflé will fall.) Fold egg whites into vegetable mixture, put in buttered 1 quart soufflé dish and bake at 350° to 375° for 25 to 30 minutes until a silver knife inserted into soufflé comes out clean. Serve immediately. Good with Hollandaise sauce (see index). Serves four.

Ratatouille

Leftover ratatouille makes a good filling for omelettes. Crumbled Feta cheese added is good too.

1 clove garlic, crushed
1 medium onion, thinly sliced
4 to 6 mushrooms, sliced
4 tbsp. olive oil
1 small eggplant, unpeeled and cubed
1 tbsp. parsley
1 bay leaf
¼ tsp. thyme
3 zucchini, thinly sliced
3 to 4 tomatoes, cut into small wedges
½ to ¾ cup grated Mozarella cheese

Heat olive oil in heavy skillet. Sauté onion and garlic until limp. Add mushrooms and sauté quickly. Add eggplant and cook on low heat stirring occasionally until eggplant is soft; about 30 minutes. Add parsley, bay leaf and thyme, mix well. Layer zucchini on top of eggplant mixture, tuck wedges of tomatoes into zucchini. Drizzle more oil over if needed. Cover and cook over low heat until zucchini is done; 15 to 20 minutes. Lift off bottom with spatula occasionally so it does not stick or burn; tomatoes and zucchini should remain in layers. Top with shredded Mozarella cheese, cover for a few minutes until cheese has melted. Serves six.

Grated Zucchini

2 large zucchini
2 tbsp. butter
$\frac{1}{8}$ tsp. nutmeg (freshly grated is best)
1 tbsp. lemon juice

Grate zucchini, heat butter until bubbly in heavy skillet, add zucchini and cook over high heat for 2 to 3 minutes, turning once or twice with a spatula. Sprinkle nutmeg on zucchini, pour on lemon juice, cover and simmer a few minutes until zucchini is cooked but still crisp. Serves four.

Zucchini Julienne Strips

3 medium zucchini
1 tbsp. finely minced onion
1 clove garlic, finely minced
2 tbsp. butter
2 tbsp. lemon juice

Cut zucchini into julienne sticks. Sauté onion and garlic quickly in butter, turn up heat, add zucchini and cook, stirring, for 2 minutes. Add lemon juice, cover and simmer until zucchini is cooked but still crisp; 5 minutes. Serves four.

Fried Carrots

6 carrots
3 tbsp. butter
freshly ground pepper

Pare carrots and cut into thin strips 3 to 4 inches long. In a heavy skillet, heat the butter until bubbly. Add carrots and stir a few minutes until coated. Grind pepper over them and cover. Stir occasionally, cooking until carrots are browned and sauce is thickened; about 15 minutes. Serves two to three.

Glazed Onions

16 medium boiling onions or
   4 medium white onions
3 tbsp. butter
2 to 3 tsp. brown sugar

Cook onions in boiling water until tender. Set aside until ready to use. Heat butter in saucepan until foamy. Add onions and stir to coat. Add brown sugar and cook slowly, stirring occasionally until sugar has melted and sauce is blended; 5 to 10 minutes. Coat onions with sauce. Serves four.

Tomatoes with Shallots

4 tomatoes
2 tbsp. butter
1 to 2 tsp. shallots or chives, finely chopped

Blanch and peel tomatoes, cut into quarters. Heat butter in saucepan. Sauté shallots. Add tomatoes stirring once, sauté until tomatoes are warmed; 1 to 3 minutes. Do not overcook. Serves four.

Fried Eggplant or Zucchini

Cut the vegetable as for French fries; ½ to ¾ inches thick and 5 to 6 inches long. (Peel eggplant if that's what you're using, but not the zucchini.) Dip in beaten egg and coat with bread crumbs. Deep fry at 375° until golden. This is also good as an appetizer.

Sauce for Artichokes

½ cup mayonnaise
2 tsp. prepared Dijon mustard
2 tsp. lemon juice

Blend together and serve with hot or cold artichokes.

Beer Batter for Fried Vegetables

onion rings, cut ¾ to 1 inch thick
mushrooms, halved
cooked artichoke hearts, halved
¾ cup flour
1 tsp. salt
1 tsp. paprika
½ tsp. baking powder
¾ cup beer

Sift together flour, salt, paprika, and baking powder. Add beer and beat well until smooth. Let sit for 5 to 10 minutes. Dip vegetables in batter, deep fry in 375° oil until golden brown on both sides. Drain on paper towels and lightly salt. Keep warm in the oven or reheat on a cookie sheet in a 400° oven until crisp. Recipe can be doubled for larger amounts.

Potato Pancakes

2½ cups coarsely grated raw potato
1 small onion, grated
1 tsp. salt
2 to 3 tbsp. flour
1 tbsp. melted bacon grease
1 beaten egg
4 or more tbsp. bacon grease for frying

Peel potatoes. Place them in cold water until ready to grate.

Mix grated potatoes and onion with flour and salt. Add beaten egg and melted bacon grease and mix well. Heat remaining bacon grease in a heavy skillet. Spoon in small mounds of potato mixture, flatten with a spatula and fry to a golden brown on both sides. Keep pancakes in oven until ready to serve. They can be reheated on a cookie sheet in the oven.

Potatoes

Potato Balls

Use a large melon baller to cut balls from a small potato. In a heavy skillet heat 2 tbsp. butter and a few drops of oil. Brown potatoes to golden on all sides, sprinkle with salt and freshly ground pepper, cover and cook, stirring occasionally, until potatoes are tender.

Oven Fried Potatoes

Peel potatoes and cut into small cubes. Melt ¼ cup margarine in a shallow baking pan in a 375° oven. When melted, add potatoes, toss to coat, sprinkle with onion salt and bake stirring occasionally for 30 minutes or until crisp.

Stuffed Baked Potatoes

Wash and dry potatoes. Prick the skin with a fork and bake for 1 hour at 400.° Cut in half lengthwise, scoop out insides into a bowl. Mash with a little milk and butter, add salt and pepper to taste. Return to shell, top with 1 tbsp. grated Cheddar cheese, return to oven and bake until cheese melts.

French Fried Potatoes

Peel potatoes and cut into ¼ to ½ inch strips. Cover with cold water, let stand 15 minutes. Drain thoroughly and dry. Cook in 350° to 375° hot oil for 4 to 6 minutes, remove before brown. Drain on paper towel. When ready to serve, refry in hot oil until golden brown. The double frying keeps them from getting soggy and too soft on the inside.

Potato Casserole
This is good to have for a group and can
be made ahead.

8 medium potatoes
1 bay leaf
4 tbsp. butter
1 can cream of chicken soup
1½ cups sour cream
¼ tsp. salt
3 green onions, chopped (tops too)
2 cups grated Cheddar cheese

Put unpeeled potatoes in boiling water with bay leaf and boil until barely tender. Cool. Peel and coarsely grate.

Stir melted butter into soup. Add sour cream and stir until smooth. Stir in green onions, 1½ cups grated cheese and salt. Pour over potatoes and mix gently. Spoon into buttered 2½-quart casserole or pan. Bake uncovered at 350° for 30 minutes. Sprinkle top with remaining cheese and bake 10 to 15 minutes longer. Serves ten to twelve.

Sauces for a Spaghetti Side Dish

Fresh Tomato Sauce

3 large tomatoes
½ tsp. tarragon
½ tsp. sweet basil
½ tsp. chives
¼ tsp. salt
¼ tsp. ground pepper

Peel and chop tomatoes. (Blanch tomatoes by pouring boiling water over them for easy peeling.) Heat butter in saucepan until foamy, add tomatoes and spices. Cook, stirring occasionally, until thick; 5 to 10 minutes. Drain spaghetti, toss with 1 tbsp. butter, add sauce and toss again. Top with grated Parmesan cheese. Serves four as a side dish or two for lunch.

Butter and Garlic Sauce

2 tbsp. olive oil
1 clove garlic, finely minced
5 tbsp. butter
3 tbsp. grated Parmesan cheese

Heat olive oil in saucepan, sauté garlic in oil (do not brown). Add butter and melt, simmer a few minutes to blend. Drain spaghetti, pour on sauce and toss. Add cheese and toss again. Serves two.

Red Cabbage

½ medium head red cabbage
2 tbsp. butter
3 tbsp. apple cider vinegar
1 tbsp. dry red wine
3 tbsp. sugar
½ tsp. salt
¼ cup water
pinch of cinnamon

Discard tough outer leaves of cabbage. Shred finely. Put the rest of the ingredients in a heavy pan or Dutch oven, bring to a boil, simmer for 2 minutes. Add cabbage, stir to coat well, cover and simmer, stirring occasionally for 25 minutes. Serves four.

Glazed Beets

1 can small beets (1 lb.)
½ cup beet liquid
⅓ cup cider vinegar
½ cup brown sugar
3 bay leaves
¼ tsp. salt
¼ tsp. cinnamon
¼ tsp. cloves
2 tbsp. cornstarch blended with ¼ cup beet liquid

Mix beet liquid, vinegar, sugar and spices in a saucepan. Bring to a boil. Add cornstarch mixed with beet liquid and simmer 10 minutes, stirring constantly. Add beets and heat thoroughly. Serve hot or cold. Serves four or five.

Easy Pesto
This is a quick pesto made from dried
instead of fresh herbs.

4 tbsp. butter
4 tbsp. olive oil
1 clove garlic, finely minced
¼ tsp. salt
1 tbsp. parsley
1 tbsp. plus 2 tsp. dried sweet basil
3 tbsp. grated Parmesan cheese

In a small saucepan, heat olive oil, quickly sauté
garlic (be careful not to brown) add butter, salt, parsley
and basil. Heat and stir until butter has melted and
ingredients are well blended. Remove from heat and
let sit for 15 minutes. Reheat, stir in cheese and mix
well. Serve over thin noodles. Serves four.

VEGETABLES

VEGETABLES

VEGETABLES

Cheese Bread

Try this toasted.

1 package dry yeast
¼ cup warm water
1 cup milk
1 tbsp. sugar
1 tsp. salt
1 tbsp. shortening
3¾ cups flour
1 egg
1 cup grated Cheddar cheese

Soften yeast in water. Scald milk, (heat on low until skin forms, do not boil) add sugar, salt and shortening and cool to lukewarm. Stir in 1 cup of flour, egg and cheese. Add yeast and beat well. Add remaining flour (it will be a moderately stiff dough). Turn onto lightly floured board and knead until smooth and elastic; about 8 minutes. Let rise, covered in bowl until doubled; about 1½ hours.

Punch down and let rest 10 minutes. Shape into loaf and put in greased loaf pan. Cover and let rise until double in bulk; about 45 minutes. Bake at 375° for 20 to 30 minutes.

Herb Bread

This bread is very good toasted and served with omelets or used to make grilled Swiss cheese sandwiches. It can also be made into bread sticks.

1 ¼ cups warm water (110°)
1 package dry yeast
2 tbsp. sugar
2 tsp. salt
2 tbsp. soft butter
2 tsp. chives
2 tsp. parsley
1 tsp. dill
3 ¾ cups unsifted flour

Put warm water into a warmed mixing bowl, sprinkle in yeast and stir until dissolved. Add sugar, salt, butter, herbs and 1½ cups flour. Beat 2 minutes at medium speed, mixing well. Stir in remaining flour and mix until smooth. Cover and let rise in a warm place until double in bulk; 30 to 40 minutes.

Punch down and lightly knead until smooth and elastic; 5 to 6 minutes. (This is a very soft dough.) Shape into loaf and place in greased 9″ by 5″ loaf pan. Cover and let rise until double in bulk; 40 to 60 minutes. Bake at 375° for 45 to 55 minutes.

Bread Sticks

Roll dough into a rectangle about ½ inch thick. Cut into strips. Roll lightly between your hands until a "stick" is formed between 8 to 10 inches long. Brush tops with vegetable oil, cover and let rise until doubled. Bake at 400° for 10 to 15 minutes.

Pita Bread

This is a Middle Eastern bread that puffs up to form a pocket when baked.

3 cups unbleached white flour
1 package dry yeast
1 tsp. salt
1 cup lukewarm water

Sift flour and salt into a large bowl, add yeast and mix. Pour water in gradually, mixing with a fork. Mix together until dough pulls away from side of bowl. Cover and let rise in a warm place until double in bulk; 1 hour.

Knead on a lightly floured surface for 3 to 4 minutes. Separate into 9 or 10 balls. Roll balls into thin rounds. Put on ungreased cookie sheet, cover and let sit at room temperature for 20 minutes. Bake at 450° for 6 to 8 minutes until top puffs. These do not get brown. Store in plastic bag.

Sopaipillas

Sopaipillas are a Southwestern puffed fried bread.

4 cups flour
4 tsp. baking powder
¼ cup shortening
2 tsp. salt
water

Sift dry ingredients into a large bowl. Cut in shortening with fork or pastry blender. Add a little water (just enough to hold dough together) and knead for a few minutes. Roll out very thin on a lightly floured board (start with a rectangle rather than a circle.) Cut into 3 inch squares. Fry to a golden brown in hot oil. They will puff up. Slit top open and serve with honey butter.

Honey butter

Cream equal amounts of honey and butter together until light and fluffy.

Popovers

1 cup milk
3 eggs
1 tbsp. vegetable oil
1 cup flour
½ tsp. salt

Beat eggs, milk and oil together with a rotary beater. Sift in flour and salt, beat until smooth. Fill well-greased deep muffin tins or custard cups ½ full. Bake at 425° for 35 minutes.

Bran Muffins

These muffins are good for breakfast. The batter will keep in the refrigerator for two weeks.

2 cups stoneground whole wheat flour
1 cup bran cereal
2 tsp. baking powder
2 tsp. soda
1 tsp. salt
1 cup sugar
¾ cup vegetable oil
2 cups milk
2 eggs, well beaten
¾ cup raisins or cut-up dates

Mix dry ingredients, including sugar, in a large bowl. Stir in oil, milk and eggs, mixing well. Add raisins. Put in covered container in refrigerator overnight. Do not freeze.

Fill greased muffin tins (or use paper baking cups) half full. Bake at 375° for 15 minutes.

Baking Powder Biscuits

2 cups flour
½ tsp. salt
3 tsp. baking powder
4 tbsp. shortening
⅔ cup milk

Sift dry ingredients together. Cut in shortening with a fork or pastry blender until crumbly. Add milk and stir with fork just until dough stays together. Put on a lightly floured board and pat until ½ inch thick. Cut with round biscuit cutter and place on ungreased cookie sheet. Bake at 450° for 12 to 15 minutes.

Corn Bread

1 cup flour
1 cup corn meal
2 tsp. sugar
4 tsp. baking powder
⅓ cup soft margarine or shortening
¾ tsp. salt
1 beaten egg
1 cup milk

Mix flour, corn meal, sugar, baking powder and salt together. Cut in shortening with a fork or pastry blender until crumbly. Add egg to milk and quickly stir into flour mixture. Stir just enough to blend ingredients. Pour into greased 8 or 9 inch square baking pan and bake at 400° for 25 minutes. This can also be made into muffins. Bake at 425° for 20 minutes.

Brown Bread

1 cup flour
1 cup graham flour (whole wheat)
1 cup whole wheat flour
½ cup brown sugar
1 tsp. salt
½ cup molasses
1 cup raisins
   or ½ cup raisins and ½ cup chopped nuts
2 cups sour milk
   (or 2 cups milk plus 2½ tbsp. vinegar to sour)
2 scant tsp. soda

Mix the flours, brown sugar and salt together in a large bowl. Stir in molasses. Mix soda and milk, and add to batter. Blend well. Stir in raisins and nuts (if used). Fill one greased loaf pan ¾ full. Let sit for 1 hour, bake at 350° for 1 hour.

Zucchini Bread

3 eggs
1 cup vegetable oil
2 cups brown sugar
2 cups grated, unpeeled zucchini
2 tsp. vanilla
3 cups whole wheat flour
3 tsp. cinnamon
1 tsp. soda
1 tsp. salt
½ tsp. baking powder
½ cup chopped walnuts

Combine eggs, oil, sugar and vanilla. Mix well. Add zucchini and blend. Do not overstir.

Sift together dry ingredients and stir into zucchini batter. Fold in walnuts. Pour into a greased loaf pan and bake 1 hour at 325°.

Pumpkin Bread

3½ cups sifted flour
2 tsp. baking soda
1½ tsp. salt
1 tsp. nutmeg
1 tsp. cinnamon
3 cups sugar
1 cup oil
4 eggs
¾ cup water
2 cups pumpkin
1 cup chopped walnuts
1 cup raisins (optional)

Mix dry ingredients in a large bowl. In a smaller bowl, mix oil, eggs and water until blended. Make a well in the flour mixture and stir in liquid, a little at a time until blended. Add pumpkin, nuts and raisins and stir until thoroughly combined. Pour batter into three small greased and floured loaf pans ¾ full or less. Bake at 350° for 1 hour.

Banana Nut Bread

5 tbsp. butter
5 tbsp. shortening
⅔ cup sugar
1 cup mashed ripe bananas
2 eggs
⅓ cup buttermilk
2¼ cups flour
1 tsp. soda
½ to ⅔ cup chopped pecans or walnuts

Cream butter and shortening together with sugar until light and fluffy. Stir in bananas and eggs, add milk and mix thoroughly. Sift in flour and soda together and mix until creamy. Fold in nuts. Pour into a greased 9″ by 5″ loaf pan and bake at 350° for 55 to 60 minutes.

Orange Bread
This bread is good buttered and grilled.

peel of 2 oranges (remove any white)
¾ to 1 cup water
⅞ cup sugar
1 tbsp. butter
1 cup sugar
2 cups graham flour (whole wheat)
2 cups white flour
4 tsp. baking powder
½ tsp. salt
1 cup orange juice (from the 2 oranges)
   If there is less than one cup of juice
   make up the difference with milk.
   Do not mix them together.
1 cup milk
1 egg

Cook orange peel in a small saucepan with water to cover until tender; 10 to 12 minutes. Add sugar and simmer until syrupy; 15 to 20 minutes. Cool.

Cream butter and sugar together, beat in egg. Mix baking powder and salt with flours. Add flour alternately with milk. Grind orange peel mixture in a food chopper and add to batter. Pour into two medium greased loaf pans, let stand for 20 minutes. Bake 1 hour at 325°.

Holiday Coffee Cake

This can be made ahead and frozen.

¼ cup sugar
1 tsp. salt
¼ cup shortening
1 cup lukewarm milk
1 package dry yeast
1 egg
3½ to 3¾ cups sifted flour
½ cup melted butter
½ cup brown sugar
¼ cup granulated sugar
1 tsp. cinnamon

Mix together in a large bowl sugar, shortening and milk. Add yeast and stir until dissolved. Stir in egg. Mix in flour in two additions, first with a wooden spoon and then with your hands. Add enough flour to make dough easy to handle.

Put dough on a lightly floured board, cover and let rest for 10 minutes. Knead until smooth and elastic. Put in greased bowl, cover and let rise until double in bulk; about 1½ hours.

Punch down, cover and let rise until not quite double in bulk; about 30 minutes. Punch down again, cover and let rest for 15 minutes.

Cut into walnut-sized pieces and form into small balls. Roll each ball in melted butter and then into mixed sugars and cinnamon. Grease a 9-inch tube cake pan and layer balls, barely touching. Cover and let rise until double in bulk; about 45 minutes. Bake at 375° for 35 to 40 minutes. Break apart to serve.

Orange Twist Rolls

¼ cup warm water (110°)
1 package dry yeast
½ cup milk
¼ cup shortening
3 tbsp. sugar
½ tsp. salt
2½ to 3 cups flour
1 beaten egg
1½ tbsp. grated orange rind
2 tbsp. orange juice

Sprinkle yeast into warm water in a small bowl. In a small saucepan scald milk (heat until bubbles form on the edge, do not boil). Add shortening, sugar and salt to milk. Pour into a large bowl and cool until luke-warm.

Stir 1 cup of flour into milk mixture, and beat well; add egg, mix well. Stir in yeast, orange juice, rind and remaining flour to make a soft dough. Cover and let rest for 10 minutes.

Knead dough on lightly floured board until smooth and elastic; 8 to 10 minutes. Cover and let rise in a warm place until double in bulk; about 2 hours. Punch down and let rest for 10 minutes.

Roll dough into rectangle ¼ inch thick. Cut into strips 4 inches long, ½ inch wide. Roll each strip lightly between your hands. Loosely tie the dough into a single knot. Place on greased cookie sheet, cover and let rise until almost doubled; about 45 minutes. Bake at 400° for 12 minutes or until done. Ice with orange icing. These can be frozen before icing.

Orange Icing

1 tsp. grated orange rind
2 tbsp. orange juice
1 cup powdered sugar

Sift sugar into a small bowl, add orange juice and rind and mix well. Use a pastry brush to brush icing on rolls for a smooth glaze.

An easy way to find if dough has doubled is to press two fingers ½ inch deep into dough. If holes remain, the dough has doubled.

Bread can be baked in coffee cans filled half full for round loaves.

BREAD

BREAD

BREAD

BREAD

BREAD

cakes & cookies

Chocolate Cake

¾ cup butter
1¾ cups sugar
2 eggs
1 tsp. vanilla
2 cups flour
¾ cup cocoa
1¼ tsp. soda
1⅓ cups water

Cream butter and sugar until light and fluffy. Add eggs and vanilla and beat for 1 minute. Combine dry ingredients, sift alternately with water. Pour into greased and floured 8 inch cake pans. (9 inch pans are too big for this batter. The cake will come out thin.) Bake at 350° for 35 to 40 minutes. Frost with either easy chocolate frosting or penuche frosting (see index).

Chocolate Orange Cake

8 oz. pitted dates, cut up
1¼ cups orange juice
1 tsp. grated orange rind
½ cup shortening
⅔ cup sugar
2 eggs, lightly beaten
1 tsp. vanilla
1 cup flour (unsifted)
1 tsp. salt
1 tsp. soda
1 tbsp. cocoa

Topping

⅔ cup semisweet chocolate chips
½ to ⅔ cup chopped walnuts

In a small saucepan bring orange juice to a boil, add dates and orange rind, cook 1 minute. Set aside to cool.

Cream shortening and sugar until light, add eggs and vanilla and beat until light. Sift flour, salt, soda and cocoa together into batter, beat until smooth and thick. Pour in the orange juice/date mixture and blend. (Do not beat too much, the dates should not be mashed.) Put into a greased 9" by 9" baking pan, sprinkle the chocolate chips and nuts on top, pressing them very lightly into batter. Bake at 325° for 35 to 40 minutes. Cool before serving.

The chocolate/nut topping can be left off and cream cheese frosting used instead (see index).

Rich Yellow Cake

½ cup shortening
1½ cups sugar
1 cup milk
2 cups flour
½ tsp. salt
3 tsp. baking powder
1 tsp. vanilla
1 tsp. lemon flavoring
3 eggs

Cream shortening and sugar in a large bowl. Sift flour, baking powder and salt together onto wax paper, put back into sifter. Sift ⅓ of flour into batter and mix well. Add milk alternately with remaining flour. Add flavorings. Beat eggs into batter until light. Bake in a greased 9″ by 12″ baking pan at 350° for 30 minutes. Frost cake with plain icing, chocolate frosting (see index) or pour lemon glaze over it.

Lemon Glaze

juice and grated rind of 2 lemons
2 cups powdered sugar

Sift sugar into medium bowl, add grated lemon rind and juice, stir until well blended. Punch holes in cake while still warm and drizzle icing over it. Let it sit in the pan for several hours for the cake to absorb the glaze.

Cassata

1 loaf pound cake
2 cups ricotta cheese (1 lb.)
2 tbsp. whipping cream
6 tbsp. powdered sugar
or
1 cup whipping cream
6 tbsp. powdered sugar
3 tbsp. finely chopped candied orange peel
4 squares semisweet chocolate, coarsely chopped
3 tbsp. Cointreau or orange flavored liqueur

Chill pound cake for an hour so it will cut easily. Slice the cake horizontally into three ½ inch layers.

Force cheese through a sieve into a bowl. Add 2 tbsp. cream, sugar and Cointreau. Beat until smooth. (If using whipping cream, whip until fairly stiff.) Fold chopped chocolate and orange peel into mixture until evenly distributed.

Spread bottom layer of cake with half of mixture, put the next layer on top, spread with remaining mixture and put on the top layer. Press the layers together. Wrap and chill in the refrigerator for 24 hours. Frost with chocolate orange frosting or with sweetened whipped cream and chocolate curls.

Frosting

3 tbsp. butter
5 squares semisweet chocolate
1 tbsp. Cointreau or orange flavored liqueur

Melt butter and chocolate in a saucepan over low heat, remove from heat. Add Cointreau, stirring until thick. This is a thin coating, double it if you prefer a thicker frosting on the cake.

Pound Cake

This is really a "half pound" cake. The recipe can easily be doubled for a large cake. If doubled, bake in a greased 9 inch tube pan at 350° for 1 hour.

½ lb. butter
½ lb. powdered sugar (2 cups, unsifted)
½ lb. flour (2 cups, unsifted)
3 eggs
2 tsp. vanilla

Cream butter until soft. Sift in powdered sugar and cream until fluffy. Add eggs one at a time, beating well after each addition. Sift in flour and mix well. Add vanilla and beat well. The batter will be very thick. Pour into greased 9" by 5" loaf pan. Bake at 350° for 1 hour.

Spiced Prune Cake

¾ cup pitted prunes
water to cover prunes
1 scant cup shortening
1 cup sugar
2 eggs
1½ cups flour
1¼ tsp. soda
1 tsp. cinnamon
½ tsp. cloves
½ tsp. salt
½ cup sour milk (or ½ cup milk and
   2 tsp. vinegar to sour)

Put prunes in a saucepan with water to cover. Bring to a boil. Turn heat down, cover and simmer until tender and plump; 15 to 20 minutes. Drain prunes and cut into pieces to make 1 cup.

Cream shortening and sugar until light. Add eggs and beat well. Sift dry ingredients together and add alternately with milk. Beat until well mixed. Stir in prunes, mix well. Bake in greased 9″ by 12″ baking pan at 350° for 25 to 30 minutes. Frost with plain icing or cream cheese frosting (see index).

Blueberry Cake

1 cup sugar
½ cup butter
3 eggs
2 cups flour
1 tsp. cinnamon
½ tsp. cloves
½ tsp. soda
1 scant tsp. baking powder
5 tsp. sour milk (or 5 tsp. milk and
    1 tsp. vinegar to sour)
1 tsp. vanilla
1 cup blueberries and liquid

Cream butter and sugar until light, add eggs one at a time, beating well after each addition. Add milk and vanilla and beat well. Sift dry ingredients together and add to batter. Beat until well blended. Stir in blueberries and juice. Pour into greased 9" by 12" pan and bake at 350° for 1 hour. This is especially good served warm with whipped cream.

Orange Cake

½ cup butter or margarine
1 cup sugar
2 eggs
1 tsp. vanilla
2 cups flour
¼ tsp. salt
2 tsp. grated orange rind
¾ cup buttermilk
1 scant tsp. soda

Combine butter and sugar together until light. Add eggs, one at a time, beating well after each addition. Add vanilla and orange rind. Mix soda with buttermilk. Sift flour and salt together and add alternately with buttermilk. Beat well. Bake in greased 9" by 9" baking pan at 350° for 30 to 35 minutes. Cool.

Glaze

1 cup sugar
⅔ cup orange juice
2 tbsp. lemon juice
2 tbsp. butter

Heat all ingredients together until well blended. Cool 30 minutes before using. With a toothpick make many holes in the top of cake and pour glaze on cake. It will seep in. Let cake sit for several hours.

Carrot Cake

1 cup sugar
¾ cup Wesson oil
2 eggs
1 tsp. vanilla
1 cup flour
1½ tsp. cinnamon
¼ tsp. nutmeg (optional)
1 tsp. soda
½ tsp. salt
1½ cups grated carrots
⅔ cup chopped walnuts

Mix sugar, oil, eggs and vanilla in a large mixing bowl. Beat until well blended. Sift in flour, cinnamon, soda and salt together. Beat until thick. Stir in carrots and nuts. Bake in a greased 9″ by 9″ baking pan at 350° for 30 to 35 minutes. Frost with one half recipe of cream cheese frosting (see index).

Coffee Cake

2 eggs
1 scant cup sugar
¾ cup melted shortening
1 scant cup milk
2¼ cups sifted flour
1½ tsp. baking powder
1 tsp. salt
3 to 4 tsp. lemon flavoring

Topping

¾ cup firmly packed brown sugar
2 tbsp. sugar
1 tsp. cinnamon
5 tbsp. melted butter

Beat eggs until light, cream in sugar. Add melted shortening and mix well. Sift flour, baking powder and salt together. Add alternately with milk. Beat well. Add lemon flavoring and mix. Pour into greased 9" by 12" baking pan.

Melt butter and pour over top of batter, spreading evenly with a knife. In a small bowl mix brown sugar, sugar and cinnamon together, sprinkle on top of batter. Bake at 375° for 25 to 35 minutes.

Creamy Chocolate Frosting

6 tbsp. butter
2 scant cups powdered sugar
1 well beaten egg
2 squares unsweetened chocolate
½ tsp. vanilla

Cream butter until light. Gradually sift in sugar, beating until creamy. Add beaten egg and beat until smooth. Melt chocolate on very low heat and beat into sugar mixture. Beat until light and thick. Add vanilla, beat well. Frosts one layer cake.

Quick Chocolate Frosting

2½ squares unsweetened chocolate
2 tbsp. butter
3 tbsp. milk
2 cups powdered sugar
dash of salt
½ tsp. vanilla

Melt chocolate and butter in a small saucepan over low heat. Add milk. Stir once or twice and remove from heat. Pour chocolate mixture into sifted sugar and salt. Beat until creamy. Add vanilla. If the frosting is too stiff, add a few drops of milk. If too thin, add a little more sugar. Frosts one layer cake.

Coffee Chocolate Frosting

2 cups powdered sugar
4 tbsp. cocoa
4 tbsp. butter
4 tbsp. strong hot coffee
1 tsp. vanilla

Sift sugar and cocoa together. Cream in butter. Add hot coffee and beat until thick and smooth. Beat in vanilla. If the frosting is too stiff add a few drops of coffee, if too thin, add more sugar. Frosts one layer cake.

Penuche Frosting

⅓ cup butter
⅔ cup brown sugar
3 tbsp. milk
1 to 1½ cups sifted, powdered sugar

Melt butter in saucepan. Stir in brown sugar. Bring to a boil and cook stirring constantly over low heat for 2 minutes. Stir in milk, bring to a boil, stirring constantly. Remove from heat and cool to luke warm (120°). Sift in powdered sugar and beat until thick and of spreading consistency.

Butter Cream Frosting

2 cups powdered sugar
5 tbsp. soft butter
3 tbsp. milk
1 tsp. vanilla

Sift sugar into large bowl. Cream in butter until well blended. Add milk and beat until creamy and fluffy. Add vanilla and beat until smooth. Frosts one layer cake. If you add a little less milk, this will be stiff enough to use for cake decorating.

Plain Icing

2 tbsp. milk
2 tbsp. butter
2 cups powdered sugar
½ tsp. vanilla

Melt milk and butter in a small saucepan over low heat. Add to sifted powdered sugar gradually, beating constantly, until smooth and creamy. Beat in vanilla. Frosts one 9" by 12" sheet cake.

Cream Cheese Frosting

6 oz. cream cheese
4 tbsp. soft butter
2 to 2½ cups powdered sugar
1 tsp. vanilla

Cream butter and cream cheese until well blended. Sift in powdered sugar and beat at high speed until light and creamy. Add vanilla and blend. Be sure the cake is completely cooled before frosting or the frosting will melt into it. Frosts one layer cake.

Naomi's Bars

4 cups oatmeal
1 cup brown sugar
½ cup light corn syrup
3 tsp. vanilla
⅔ cup butter

Mix oatmeal and sugar in a large bowl. Melt butter over low heat and blend in corn syrup and vanilla. Mix into oatmeal and sugar. Spread in greased 9" by 12" baking pan. Bake 12 minutes at 375°.Cool.

Topping

1 package semisweet chocolate chips (12 oz.)
⅔ cup chunky peanut butter

Melt chocolate chips in double boiler or over very low heat. Stir in peanut butter and blend. Spread on cooled oatmeal mixture. Regfrigerate until firm. Cut into small squares; these are very rich.

Brownies

4 squares unsweetened chocolate
1 cup butter
2 cups sugar
3 eggs, beaten until light
1 tsp. vanilla
1 cup sifted flour
¼ tsp. salt

Melt chocolate and butter in double boiler or over low heat. Mix sugar, eggs and vanilla well, add chocolate/butter mixture, mix well. Add dry ingredients (sifted together), beat until smooth. Pour into greased and floured 9″ by 12″ baking pan. Bake at 350° for 35 minutes.

Chocolate Ice Box Cookies

⅔ cup shortening
1½ cups sugar
2 squares unsweetened chocolate, melted
1 egg
⅓ cup milk
2½ cups flour
⅓ tsp. salt
2 tsp. baking powder

Cream shortening and sugar. Add egg, milk and melted chocolate, mixing well. Sift dry ingredients together into batter. Form into a roll, wrap in wax paper and chill. Slice thinly and bake on ungreased cookie sheet for 8 to 10 minutes at 350.°

Oatmeal Chocolate Chip Cookies

This recipe makes a large amount; the uncooked dough freezes well.

½ **lb. margarine**
2 lbs. brown sugar
3 large eggs
1 tsp. vanilla
2 cups flour
1 tsp. soda
1 tsp. salt
2 cups oatmeal
1 package semisweet chocolate chips (12 oz.)

Cream butter and sugar. Add eggs, beat well, add vanilla. Sift dry ingredients into batter and mix well. Stir in oatmeal and chocolate chips. Drop by spoonfuls onto ungreased cookie sheet. Bake 8 to 10 minutes at 375°. Take cookies out when they are light brown and look undercooked. Cool on wire rack.

Peanut Butter Cookies

1 cup butter or margarine
1 cup sugar
1 cup brown sugar
1 cup crunchy peanut butter
2 eggs
¼ cup milk
2 tsp. vanilla
3½ cups flour
2 tsp. soda
1 tsp. salt

Cream butter and sugar until light. Mix in peanut butter. Beat in eggs, milk and vanilla. Sift dry ingredients together into batter. Roll into balls and roll balls in sugar. Bake 10 to 12 minutes at 375°.

A variation of these: Put a chocolate star or kiss in the center of each cookie and press in before baking.

Ginger Snaps

¾ cup shortening
1 cup sugar
¼ cup molasses
1 beaten egg
2 cups flour
¼ tsp. salt
2 tsp. soda
1 tsp. cinnamon
1 tsp. cloves
1½ tsp. ginger

Cream shortening and sugar until light. Add molasses and beaten egg. Sift dry ingredients together into batter and mix well. Roll into walnut sized balls and roll in sugar. Place on ungreased cookie sheet and bake at 350° for 12 to 15 minutes. The balls can be frozen, unsugared in a plastic bag and used as needed.

Almond Christmas Cookies

½ cup shortening
½ cup butter
⅓ cup sugar
⅔ cup blanched, ground almonds
1⅔ cups sifted flour
¼ tsp. salt
1 cup powdered sugar
1 tsp. cinnamon

Cream butter, shortening and sugar until light. Mix in almonds. Sift salt and flour into mixture and work in until well blended. Form into a roll, wrap in wax paper and chill. Slice ¼ inch thick and bake at 325° for 14 to 16 minutes on ungreased cookie sheet. Mix powdered sugar and cinnamon together. While cookies are still warm, roll into powdered sugar.

Sugar Cookies

1 cup shortening
1½ cups sugar
2 eggs
3 cups flour
1 tsp. salt
1 tsp. soda
1 tsp. dried grated orange or lemon peel (optional)
¾ cup sour milk (or ¾ cup milk and
   2 tsp. vinegar to sour)
1 tsp. vanilla

Cream shortening and sugar until light and fluffy. Add eggs and beat well. Sift dry ingredients together and mix alternately with milk. Add vanilla and beat well. If dough is too soft, chill 1 hour before rolling. Roll out on lightly floured board and cut with cookie cutters. Bake on cookie sheet at 350° for 12 to 15 minutes.

Shortbread

½ cup butter
1 package cream cheese (3 oz.)
¼ cup sugar
1 tsp. vanilla
1¼ cups sifted flour

Cream butter and cream cheese until light. Add sugar and vanilla and cream until fluffy. Add flour and mix well. Roll out on lightly floured board and cut with cookie cutters or into oblong shapes. Bake at 300° for 30 to 35 minutes.

Fudge Pudding Cake

A chocolate sauce forms under this cake when baked.

1 cup flour
1 tsp. baking powder
½ tsp. salt
¾ cup sugar
2 tbsp. cocoa
½ cup milk
1 tsp. vanilla
2 tbsp. melted shortening

Topping

4 tbsp. cocoa
¾ cup brown sugar
1¾ cups hot water

Sift flour, baking powder, salt, sugar and 2 tbsp. cocoa together. Combine milk, vanilla and shortening and mix into dry ingredients. Pour into a greased 9 inch square baking pan. Combine brown sugar, 4 tbsp. cocoa and sprinkle over batter. Carefully pour hot water over uncooked batter and bake at 350° for 40 minutes.

Serve while still warm with whipped cream or ice cream.

Chocolate Roll

3 eggs
⅞ cup sugar
¾ cup flour
½ cup cocoa
½ tsp. salt
1¼ tsp. baking powder
¼ cup water
½ tsp. vanilla
½ tsp. lemon flavoring
¼ cup powdered sugar

Preheat oven to 450°.

Beat eggs until light and creamy. Add ⅞ cup sugar and mix. Add flavorings to water and sift dry ingredients together. Add dry ingredients alternately with water. Beat until batter is blended.

Line a cookie sheet with parchment paper or brown paper leaving an overhanging edge. Spread batter evenly onto pan, and place in oven. Turn down to 425° and bake for 11 minutes.

Turn baked roll onto tea towel and pull paper off. Sift powdered sugar over cake and roll up like a jelly roll. Serve topped with whipped cream or vanilla ice cream and fudge sauce (see index).

Chocolate Mousse

This is simple to make (unlike the French way),
rich and creamy.

2 large eggs
2 tbsp. brandy
2 tbsp. sugar
dash of salt
1 package semisweet chocolate chips (12 oz.)
1½ cups milk

Place everything except milk, eggs first, into blender.
Scald milk. (Heat it over medium heat until film forms
on top. Do not boil.) Pour milk in blender and blend
60 seconds at lowest speed. Pour into cups and
refrigerate at least five hours until firm. Serve topped
with whipped cream sweetened with a little powdered
sugar. Serves eight.

Fudge Brownie Pie

This is a good last minute dessert; it takes only 5 minutes to mix.

2 eggs
1 cup sugar
½ cup soft butter or margarine
½ cup flour
4 tbsp. cocoa
1 tsp. vanilla
pinch of salt
½ cup chopped walnuts (optional)

Put all ingredients in a small bowl in order given, except nuts. Beat for 4 minutes. Stir in nuts (if used). Pour into a buttered pie pan and bake at 325° for 30 minutes. Serve with whipped cream or ice cream. Serves six to eight.

Chocolate Mint Pie

Crust
14 graham crackers
1 tbsp. brown sugar
4 tbsp. melted butter

Filling
1 cup butter
1 cup powdered sugar
2 squares unsweetened chocolate
2 well beaten eggs
few drops of peppermint

Crush crackers in plastic bag with rolling pin until fine. Put in bowl, mix with sugar, add melted butter. Press into pie pan with the back of a soup spoon. Bake at 400° for 5 to 6 minutes. Cool.

Cream butter until light, add sugar and cream until smooth. Add eggs, mix well. Put in melted chocolate and mix until creamy. Add peppermint. (Do not put too much in. It gets stronger as it gets cold.) Pour into cooled pie crust and refrigerate until firm.

Black Bottom Pie

If you don't wash up as you go along you'll have counters full of dirty dishes.

15 to 16 chocolate wafer cookies
4 to 5 tbsp. soft butter
2 cups milk
4 beaten egg yolks
1¼ tbsp. cornstarch
½ cup sugar
¼ tsp. salt
1½ squares unsweetened chocolate
1 tsp. vanilla
1 tbsp. unflavored gelatin
4 tbsp. cold water
4 egg whites (room temperature)
¼ tsp. cream of tartar
½ cup sugar
1½ tsp. rum
1 cup heavy cream
2 tbsp. powdered sugar
½ square unsweetened chocolate

Put cookies in plastic bag and crush fine with a rolling pin. Put in bowl, blend in butter with a fork and press in bottom of square 8 to 9 inch pan.

To make custard, mix sugar, cornstarch and well beaten egg yolks together in a saucepan. In another pan, scald milk (heat until skin forms, do not boil). Slowly add milk to egg mixture and blend with wire whisk. Cook over low heat stirring constantly until mixture thickens.

Put 1½ squares of chocolate in small bowl, pour 1 cup of custard over them and stir until chocolate is melted. Spread over cookie crust.

Soak gelatin in cold water and add to remaining custard. Mix well and set aside to cool.

After custard has cooled beat egg whites with cream of tartar until foamy. Add sugar gradually and beat until stiff. Add rum. Beat in custard mixture, blend well and pour over chocolate layer. Refrigerate at least four hours until set.

Whip cream, add powdered sugar. Spread over top of set pie. Sprinkle top with ½ square of grated chocolate.

Nut Pie
This recipe sounds strange but is delicious when made. It is a simple torte.

18 to 20 saltines
1 tsp. baking powder
½ cup chopped or ground walnuts
3 egg whites (room temperature)
1 scant cup sugar
1 tsp. vanilla

Put saltines in plastic bag and crush with rolling pin until fine. Mix with baking powder and nuts. In a separate bowl, beat egg whites until stiff but not dry. Slowly add sugar, beating. Beat until glossy. Fold nut and cracker mixture into egg whites. Add vanilla. Put into buttered 9 inch pie pan and bake at 325° for 30 to 35 minutes. Serve topped with whipped cream sweetened with a little powdered sugar.

Lemon Meringue Pie

1 cup sugar
4 tbsp. cornstarch
¼ tsp. salt
1½ cups boiling water
1 tbsp. butter
6 tbsp. lemon juice
1 tsp. grated lemon rind
3 egg yolks
2 tbsp. milk

Meringue

3 egg whites
¼ tsp. cream of tartar
5 tbsp. sugar
1 baked and cooled pie shell (see index)

Mix cornstarch, sugar and salt in a saucepan. Add boiling water gradually, stirring constantly on low heat until clear; 5 or 6 minutes. Add butter, lemon rind and juice and cook 2 minutes. Cool slightly. Beat egg yolks with milk, add to mixture and bring to boiling point. Remove from heat and cool slightly. Pour into pie shell.

Beat egg whites and cream of tartar until foamy. Slowly add sugar and beat until stiff peaks form. Spoon onto pie, sealing meringue to edge of crust and bake at 425° until lightly browned; 4 to 5 minutes. Chill in refrigerator.

Fresh Strawberry Pie

1 cooked 9 inch pastry shell (see index)
1 quart strawberries
¾ cup water
3 tbsp. cornstarch
1 cup sugar

Wash and hull strawberries saving one cup. Line cooled pastry shell with remaining berries.

Slice the cup of berries and simmer in saucepan with water for 3 or 4 minutes. Combine cornstarch and sugar and add to cooked fruit. Cook stirring until syrup is thick and clear. Cool slightly. Pour over strawberries in shell and chill until firm. Serve topped with sweetened whipped cream.

German Peach Pie

2½ cups canned peach halves (1 lb. 13 oz.)
1 cup sugar
2 eggs
2 tbsp. butter
½ to 1 tsp. cinnamon
½ to 1 cup chopped walnuts
1 unbaked pie shell (see index)

Drain peaches and place in pie shell, round side up.

Cream butter and sugar together. Beat in eggs. Pour batter over peaches and sprinkle top with cinnamon and nuts. Bake for 15 minutes at 425°, reduce heat to 325°, and bake 45 minutes longer.

Plum Pudding
Suet is beef fat; ask your butcher for it.

2 eggs
½ cup sugar
½ cup molasses
⅔ cup chopped suet
½ cup sour milk
    (or ½ cup milk plus 2 tbsp. vinegar to sour)
¼ tsp. cinnamon
¼ tsp. ginger
¼ tsp. nutmeg
1 tsp. salt
1 tsp. soda
1 tsp. baking powder
2½ cups flour
1½ to 1¾ cups cut up candied fruit
½ cup raisins

Beat eggs in a large mixing bowl. Add sugar, molasses, suet, and sour milk. Mix spices, salt, soda and baking powder into flour and sift into batter, beating well. Stir in candied fruit and raisins.

Fill molds or 1 pound coffee cans half full. Put a double layer of foil on the top and tie securely with string. Put 2½ inches of water in a large heavy kettle, place the cans upright and cover kettle. Steam for 3 hours. Replace water if necessary.

These will keep for months in the refrigerator. To reheat, steam for 10 to 15 minutes. Serve sliced, with pudding sauce.

Pudding Sauce

½ cup whipping cream
⅓ cup sugar
¼ cup butter
1 tbsp. rum or brandy

Whip cream in a bowl. In another bowl, cream sugar and butter together until light and fluffy. Fold into whipped cream. Add rum and blend.

Apple Crisp

4 apples, peeled and sliced
½ tsp. salt
¾ cup flour
1 cup brown sugar
1 tsp. cinnamon
½ cup butter

Butter a shallow baking dish and layer sliced apples into it. Sprinkle with salt. Mix flour, sugar and cinnamon together in a bowl, cut in butter with pastry blender or fork until crumbly. Sprinkle topping over apples and bake 45 minutes at 350.° Serve topped with whipped cream.

Cheese Cake

All ingredients must be at room temperature, or the cheesecake will not be light and the butter will be difficult to work into the cracker crumbs.

Crust
14 graham crackers
¼ cup soft butter
1 tbsp. brown sugar
Filling
1 lb. cream cheese
2 eggs
¾ cup sugar
2 tsp. vanilla
½ tsp. lemon flavoring
Topping
1 cup sour cream
3½ tbsp. sugar
1 tsp. vanilla

Put crackers in plastic bag and crush with rolling pin until fine. Put into bowl, add sugar and work butter into crumbs with pastry blender or fork. Put into 9 or 10 inch pan and press into an even crust with the back of a soup spoon.

Beat softened cream cheese. Beat eggs in separate bowl and add to cream cheese. Beat until light. Add sugar, vanilla and lemon, beat until smooth. Pour into pie shell and bake at 350° for 15 to 20 minutes. Cool for 5 minutes.

Blend sour cream, sugar and vanilla. Pour over pie and bake 10 minutes at 350.° Refrigerate at least six hours.

Shortcake

1 cup flour
2 tsp. baking powder
¼ tsp. salt
2 tsp. sugar
3 tbsp. shortening
¼ cup milk
1 well beaten egg added to milk

Mix flour, baking powder, salt and sugar together in a bowl. Cut in shortening with a fork or pastry blender, until crumbly. Add egg and milk and stir well. Put on a lightly floured board and roll out to ⅓ inch thick. Cut with biscuit cutter into rounds, place two rounds on top of each other on a greased cookie sheet. Bake for 10 to 15 minutes at 450°

Split and fill with sliced, sweetened strawberries or other fruit, top with more berries and whipped cream. Serves four.

Cream Puffs

1 cup water
½ cup butter
1 cup flour
¼ tsp. salt
4 eggs

Bring water to boiling in a saucepan, add butter and stir until butter melts. When butter has melted and mixture is boiling again, add flour and salt all at once. Stir vigorously until it forms an unseparated ball. Remove from heat and cool.

Mix in eggs one at a time, stirring well after each addition. Beat with spoon until smooth.

Drop by spoonfuls on a greased cookie sheet. Bake at 450° for 15 minutes. Turn heat down to 325° and bake 25 minutes more. When cool, cut open with a sharp knife and fill with whipped cream. Frost with chocolate glaze.

Chocolate Glaze

4 squares unsweetened chocolate
¾ cup sugar
⅓ cup water

Melt chocolate in a saucepan over low heat. In another saucepan, mix sugar and water and bring to a boil. Add to chocolate, beating constantly until thick and glossy.

Schaum Torte

This uses leftover egg whites. The proportions are always ⅓ cup sugar to 1 egg white. When using egg yolks (only), whites can be frozen until needed. Mark on the container how many are in it.

4 egg whites (room temperature)
¼ tsp. cream of tartar
1⅓ cups sugar
1 tbsp. white vinegar
1 tsp. vanilla

Beat egg whites and cream of tartar until foamy. Slowly add sugar and beat until whites are stiff and stand in peaks. Add vinegar and vanilla and beat until well blended.

Drop by large spoonfuls on ungreased cookie sheet and make nest by pushing center in with small spoon. (Use meringue tip if you have a cookie press.) Bake at 275° for 45 to 60 minutes until tortes are dry and not sticky. Fill with vanilla ice cream and top with sliced, sweetened strawberries. Makes six tortes.

Dessert Crepes

2 eggs, well beaten
2 tsp. brandy
½ cup flour
2 tbsp. powdered sugar
¾ cup milk
1 tsp. melted butter

Add brandy to well beaten eggs. Sift flour into this mixture, fold in sugar alternately with milk. Add butter and beat well with an electric mixer or egg beater. This is a thin batter. Pour 2 tbsp. of batter into the center of a tilted 8 inch crepe pan, turning from side to side until the batter covers the bottom of the pan. When one side of the crepe is done (about 1 minute), turn over and cook the other side. The second side does not get very brown, and the first side is the "good" side that is used for the outside when folded. Crepes may be made ahead and stored in a plastic bag or frozen. Paper doilies are ideal to put between crepes as they are stacked. The doilies can be reused. Makes 10 crepes.

These sweet crepes are also good filled with slightly sweetened strawberries, topped with sour cream.

Crepes Suzette

½ cup butter
4 tbsp. powdered sugar
grated rind of 1 lemon
grated rind of 1 orange
juice of 1 orange
juice of ½ lemon
¼ cup Cointreau or other orange liqueur
¼ cup brandy
8 crepes

Melt butter in a heavy skillet, add lemon and orange juices and grated rinds. Bring to frothy bubble over medium heat, add sugar and heat, stirring until bubbly. Add Cointreau and simmer again to blend. Place crepes folded in fourths in pan, spooning sauce on them until they are well coated. Heat ¼ cup brandy and pour over crepes. (It will not flame unless the brandy is warm, but do not boil.) Set aflame, tilting the pan back and forth until the liqueur has burned out. Put crepes on plates, spooning any extra sauce on them and sprinkle lightly with powdered sugar. Serves four.

Bananas Flambe

6 firm bananas
6 tbsp. butter
3 tbsp. grated orange rind
3 tsp. sugar
¼ cup Curacoa or other orange flavored liqueur
¾ cup whipping cream

Cut bananas in half lengthwise. Put 3 tbsp. butter in two medium sized skillets. Heat until butter foams. Add half of the bananas to each pan. (Do not crowd or they will be hard to turn over.) Brown bananas on both sides, putting the cut side up first. Do not overcook. Sprinkle with peel and sugar. Warm Curacoa (do not boil). Pour over bananas and flame. Place two halves on each plate, spoon sauce over them and top with slightly sweetened whipped cream. Do not whip the cream stiff, just enough to hold its shape. Serves six.

These can easily be made for two or four using 3 tbsp. butter for each pan, ½ tbsp. orange rind and ½ tsp. sugar for each banana and 2 tbsp. liqueur to flame each pan.

Here are two quick fruit desserts:

Peaches with Sour Cream

1 can peach halves (1 lb. 13 oz.)
½ pint sour cream
½ tsp. nutmeg

Drain peaches, place round side up in a pie pan or shallow glass pan, pour on the sour cream and sprinkle nutmeg on top. Refrigerate for at least two hours.

Grapes in Sour Cream
This is very good with a brunch or for a light dessert.

1 cup seedless green grapes
2 to 3 tbsp. honey
¼ cup sour cream

Pour honey over grapes and stir to coat. Mix in sour cream and chill for 1 hour.

Pie Crust

2½ cups sifted unbleached flour
1 tsp. salt
4 tbsp. lard
3 to 4 tbsp. butter
½ cup ice water

Combine flour and salt and put in the freezer until well chilled. Cut lard into flour. Do this quickly: overhandling of flour makes the crust tough. This mixture should look like little peas.

Moisten flour mixture with ½ cup ice water. Blend quickly with a fork, mixing as little as possible. Divide into two parts, one a little larger than the other. Chill before rolling out.

Flour a piece of wax paper and rolling pin. After dough is chilled roll into a large ball, then roll out from center. This will make enough for the top and bottom of a 9 inch pie.

Butterscotch Sauce

1 egg yolk
5 tbsp. butter
4 tbsp. water
⅔ cup firmly packed brown sugar
⅓ cup light corn syrup
½ tsp. vanilla

Beat egg yolk with a wire whisk until thick and creamy. Add butter, water, sugar and corn syrup and stir well. Heat to boiling over medium heat, stirring constantly. Cook stirring until thick and syrupy; 7 to 10 minutes. Remove from heat and stir in vanilla. Stir before serving. Keep covered in the refrigerator. Makes 1½ cups.

Caramel Sauce

4 tbsp. butter
½ cup firmly packed brown sugar
1½ tsp. cornstarch
½ cup water
½ tsp. vanilla

Melt butter in a small saucepan, add sugar, remove from heat. Mix cornstarch in water until dissolved. Add sugar. Bring to a boil stirring constantly. Cook while the sauce is bubbling for 2 minutes, stirring constantly. Remove from heat, stir in vanilla. Keep covered in refrigerator. Serve over ice cream. Makes 1 cup.

Hot Fudge Sauce
This kind is chewy when put on ice cream.

2 tbsp. butter
2 squares unsweetened chocolate
1 cup sugar
dash of salt
2 tbsp. light corn syrup
⅓ cup boiling water
1 tsp. vanilla

Melt butter in a saucepan. Add chocolate and melt over low heat. Remove from heat. Stir in sugar, salt and corn syrup. Pour in the boiling water and mix well. Bring to full boil over medium heat and cook for 7 to 8 minutes without stirring. Do not cook any longer than this and do not stir. Remove from heat, stir in vanilla and serve over ice cream. Store any leftover covered in the refrigerator, reheat over low heat. If it gets sugary, stir in 1 tbsp. warm water.

Creamy Hot Fudge Sauce

3 squares unsweetened chocolate
1 can sweetened condensed milk
½ cup hot water
¼ tsp. salt
¼ cup sugar
1 tsp. vanilla

Melt chocolate over very low heat. Watch so it doesn't burn. (If you want to be safe, use a double boiler.) Stir in sweetened condensed milk and cook until very thick, stirring constantly. Add hot water, sugar and salt and cook until mixture is very smooth and as thick as you like it. Remove from heat and stir in vanilla. Serve over ice cream. Store covered in the refrigerator. Reheat over very low heat, stirring.

DESSERTS

DESSERTS

DESSERTS

DESSERTS

DESSERTS

DESSERTS

DESSERTS

Index

Roasting	Oven Temperature	Minutes Per Pound
Beef, rib	325°	20 to 25
rare	325°	25 to 30
medium	325°	30 to 35
well done	325°	25 to 30
Ham	300° to 325°	30 to 35
Lamb, leg	325° to 350°	30 to 40
Pork, loin	325°	30 to 35
Veal	300°	30 to 45
Chicken	325°	20 to 30
Duck	325°	25 to 30
Goose	300°	20 to 25
Turkey, 8 to 12 lb.	300°	20 to 25
12 to 20 lb.	300°	15 to 20

Contents of Cans

8 oz. = 1 cup
10½ to 12 oz. soup = 1¼ cups
12 oz. = 1½ cups
14 to 16 oz. = 1¾ cups
16 to 17 oz. = 2 cups
20 oz. (1 lb. 4 oz.) = 2½ cups
29 oz. (1 lb. 13 oz.) = 3½ cups
46 oz. (1 qt. 14 fl. oz.) = 5¾ cups

Weights and Measures

3 Teaspoons = 1 Tablespoon
2 Tablespoons = 1 Liquid Ounce
4 Tablespoons = ¼ Cup
5½ Tablespoons = ⅓ Cup
8 Tablespoons = ½ Cup
1 Cup = ½ Pint
2 Cups = 1 Pint
4 Cups = 1 Quart
2 Pints = 1 Quart
4 Quarts = 1 Gallon
16 Ounces = 1 Pound
¼ Cup Butter = 4 Tablespoons or ½ Cube
½ Cup Butter = ¼ Pound or 1 Cube
2 Cups Butter = 1 Pound
2 Cups Granulated Sugar = 1 Pound
2½ Cups Packed Brown Sugar = 1 Pound
4 Cups Flour = 1 Pound
4 Cups Grated Cheese = 1 Pound
4 Cups Unsifted Powdered Sugar = 1 Pound
4 Tablespoons Cocoa plus 2 Teaspoons butter = 1 Ounce
   Unsweetened Chocolate
1 Square Unsweetened Chocolate = 1 Ounce
11 Graham Crackers = 1 Cup Fine Crumbs
1 Cup Milk plus 1 Tablespoon Vinegar = 1 Cup Sour Milk
Juice of 1 Lemon = 3 to 4 Tablespoons
¼ Pound Chopped Nuts = 1 Cup